How I Left the Rat Ra

The Midlife *shift*

a memoir

Mo Issa

The Midlife Shift

Copyright © 2024 by Mo Issa. *All rights reserved.*

This is a work of fiction. Names, characters, places and incidents are products of the author's imagination or are used fictitiously and should not be construed as real. Any resemblance to actual events, locales, organisations or persons, living or dead, is entirely coincidental.

No part of this book may be used or reproduced in any manner whatsoever without written permission, except in the case of brief quotations embodied in critical articles and reviews.

KIMO
PUB
PRESS

Published by Kimo Pub Press
Printed in the United States of America.

978-1-0687572-1-1 *(paperback)*
978-1-0687572-0-4 *(ebook)*

To my father and mother, who, knowingly or not,
made me become who I must.

Table of Contents

Introduction vii

Chapter 1 – The Sleeping Volcano 4

Chapter 2 – In Times of War, I Found My Peace 18

Chapter 3 – In Search of the Miraculous 30

Chapter 4 – Unlocking the Power of Vulnerability 45

Chapter 5 – Unravelling My Identity 59

Chapter 6 – Unleashing the Power Within 74

Chapter 7 – Learning to Surrender 84

Chapter 8 – Reclaiming My Authenticity. 97

Chapter 9 – Making the Shift 108

Chapter 10 – A Fractured Lesson 119

Chapter 11 – Unearthing Deeper Revelations 129

Chapter 12 – Confronting My Spirituality 141

Chapter 13 – Accessing the Spiritual Warrior 149

Chapter 14 – Achieving Inner Peace. 158

Afterword 168

Acknowledgements 170

About the Author 171

Introduction

"Your problems have nothing to do with your heart but with your head," the doctor said.

It was May 2008 when my doctor suggested I see a psychiatrist for my malaise. What I was going through was not heart failure but panic attacks. It's true, the twelve months leading up to that point were turbulent, but I'd felt a dissatisfaction creeping into my being well before then. Somehow, the fulfilment I used to get from working at my company was drowned by the weight of responsibilities and expectations.

I still wasn't as financially free as I thought I would be when I first created my company fifteen years earlier. Yes, my earnings helped support a rich, extravagant, and busy life, but I had no safety net. Buying four Rolex watches within eighteen months wasn't making my happiness last. The more I made, the more affluent my life became. I had become enslaved not by a person or a giant corporation but by striving for money, prestige, and success.

On that night in 2008, on a hotel balcony in Lebanon, with a cigar in hand, I contemplated the doctor's words and could see, for the first time, myself split into two. First was the extroverted and successful business owner, an esteemed member of society whom everyone thought they knew and admired. Then there was the other person who no one but I knew. The person who wanted to be alone with his thoughts and had an insatiable curiosity about the mysticism of life. The person who craved a far less lavish lifestyle.

It was now apparent that the formula for living the good life I'd learned through osmosis was failing me. Striving for success, money, and prestige wasn't giving me the happiness I thought my achievements guaranteed.

I had followed the model my father had shown me—what all of his peers and what the wider Lebanese expatriate society had demonstrated regularly. A good life was about hard work, making money, taking care of your family, climbing the status ladder, and enjoying the fruits.

At the start of my adult life, I followed it so well that, together with the family and friends that I grew up with, we became the talk of the town, the envy of many, and the top of the list for any dinner or party invitation. We were wealthy, affluent, and sophisticated, all regularly criss-crossing the globe. As a result, we were dubbed the Millionaire's Club.

However, by the time the panic attacks began in 2008, I had become disillusioned, ambivalent and angry. I'd lost my zeal for my business and started questioning myself and the values under which I'd been living.

Why wasn't I happy? Why did the rest of the Millionaire's Club seem much more content than I did? These constant questions plagued me. Then, as my ruminations and reflections got more profound, I started to ask a more searching question:

What if I was living my life all wrong?

Maybe it didn't matter what other people thought of my life. Maybe it didn't even matter that I was living according to a self-imposed happiness formula. None of it matched what was true in my heart.

As we've evolved from being hunter-gatherers to more sophisticated human beings, our brains and psychological needs have grown. Today, there is an existential crisis that has left many, like me, feeling depressed, empty, and in search of meaning.

The uncomfortable truth is that we go through the first part of our lives in action mode, like rats chasing dopamine hit after dopamine hit, until a crisis beckons us to ask: "What if we are all living our lives the wrong way?"

We all need to sit up at various stages of our lives and ask ourselves if we are on our rightful, authentic paths. We so seldom do this. Instead, we allow the busyness of life to numb us into believing that we are doing fine. Without warning, we become slaves to our impulses—those desires consciously and subconsciously bestowed upon us by our genetic disposition, upbringing and environment, the constant media barrage, and the confusing signals of our bodies. The breakneck speed of today's world doesn't make it any easier on us. There are endless options on how to live and a never-ending number of gurus telling us how to become our best selves. There are also easy and accessible platforms for us to compete and compare. Unfortunately, the noise surrounding us has stopped our music's eruption from within.

We can all live happier, more content lives full of meaningful experiences and unique connections—and still leave a legacy—without the need for striving and without the running and the exhaustion that comes with it.

We can be healthy and have enough money to be free from needing other people, governments, or institutions. We can have a wonderful group of friends and family around us and feel useful by contributing to our communities without feeling pressured to live in the rat race.

First, we need to slow down, dig deeper into ourselves, and find out what we want. We must discover the obstacles that stand in our way and recognise the values we want to live by. We must then use those values to inform the kind of lives we want to live. No, it's not easy, but when we accept that struggle and discomfort are ways to grow and that doing the work on ourselves means removing the old paradigms that don't serve us anymore, we slowly install the habits that can lead us to what we truly want.

My story is not a Hollywood rags-to-riches story but rather a story of growing self-awareness. This inner journey is long and endless, but it's a human one. As Socrates said thousands of years ago, "The unexamined life is not worth living."

I got to know myself much better by removing my egoic exterior, layer after layer. I share my innermost feelings as a testament for others to see why examining our values and beliefs is imperative. These values are the springboard from which we can clarify what we want ... and then have the courage to go for it.

As I started to let go of the old values that I'd lived by, I was able to create new ones that resonated more with my authentic self. As a result, I started to live a more meaningful life aligned with my fresh set of values.

My values were now not extrinsically motivated but more intrinsically driven. Instead of success, prestige, accomplishment, and money, I now craved creativity, presence, simplicity, vulnerability, and authenticity. Instead of allowing my mind and society's influence to affect my wants, I now allowed my heart and body to lead the way. The more I expressed the depths of my soul and allowed my muted voice to speak, the better I connected with people and the world.

My self-discovery journey has been long and riddled with cul-de-sacs, where old demons pulled me into bouts of confusion, ambivalence, and mild depression. However, because I failed repeatedly, my path was being self-corrected, just like a rocket shooting from the Earth to the moon; it adjusts its trajectory slowly but surely to land on the right spot.

Through this journey, I have come to know what I stand for. I've clarified my values and have a particular worldview that has become my North Star. These guiding principles include:

1. Accepting that letting go of comfort and ease and allowing more pain and struggle in our lives means more growth, presence, and richness of life.
2. Not caring about society's whims (e.g., status and prestige) and instead focusing on having genuine connection and community.
3. Recognising that money beyond a certain point poisons the heart and that living frugally and simply results in purity and freedom.
4. Embracing the ordinary—being humble, useful, and competent—rather than the egocentric concept of trying to be extraordinary and saving the world.
5. Keeping the following mantra as a guide: *Get into action. Do what you love. Go for your goals. But detach from the results. Detach from the fruits of your actions.* We can only control our actions—not their outcomes. But

we should never—never—detach from our actions. We lose ourselves if we do.

As you follow along on my personal journey, I hope you too will come to see the value in these principles and find ways to adapt them for yourself. You deserve a life free of malaise—free of the disconnect that comes along with superficial success. But this can only be achieved through a fundamental shift in your mindset and the way you view yourself in the world. Allow me to share my experiences and learnings to guide you toward a deeper, richer, and more content life.

Chapter 1

The Sleeping Volcano

The rains were expected in Ghana. There's nothing I loved more than the start of the rainy season. The heat mellowed, and a light breeze would fill the mornings with a certain freshness in the air, as if the rains had come to clean the roads and rejuvenate our dried-up souls.

I didn't know it at the time, but everything was about to change, my life wiped clean like those roads. The values that I'd lived by were about to transform into ones that better reflected my true self.

But that would happen much later. The rains hadn't come yet.

It was early May 2007 and just past noon when the company's financial controller walked into my office. Our bank, having only recently given us a loan to increase our working capital and import more products, now demanded early repayment, without warning and contrary to our verbal agreement. Striving for more growth and revenues, I had pushed for months to get that larger loan. Now, the bank was threatening us with foreclosure unless we settled the whole amount within twenty-seven days.

"How can they do this?" I asked, staggered.

The company I'd built brick by brick over the last fifteen years was about to crumble under the weight of the bank's pressure.

"Technically they can," my colleague said.

Something in the small print, which we'd both overlooked, allowed them to do so.

"That's not what we negotiated when we switched our account to them," I said.

"This young bank executive is aggressive. He's already started on the paperwork," he said.

Heat surged through my body. I knew the bank executive in question. I'd refused to give him a kick-back during negotiations. Now he was taking his revenge.

"We can't pay our full liability immediately. It'll wipe us out," I said, my face red hot. "It would be suicide for the business."

The phone rang. I'd been expecting the bank but, when I answered, heard my wife's worried voice instead.

"Reda was in a serious car accident. He's unconscious and being transported by ambulance to Korle-Bu hospital. Please hurry."

I pictured Reda—my sweet sixteen-year-old nephew wearing his Manchester United football shirt and jumping for joy when we'd scored just a few days earlier. My legs and knees went weak as I left the office and ran to my car.

The next months were some of the most desperate of my life. Reda was in a car with three of his friends. Their family driver was at the wheel. He'd lost control while navigating a sharp bend and had hit a steel beam protruding from the roof of a building. All the passengers had emerged unscathed, but somehow the falling plank had landed on the roof of the car—right onto Reda's head. After a gruelling night at the Korle-Bu hospital, he'd then had to be air-lifted to the National Hospital for Neurology and Neurosurgery in London, where he fell into a coma for several weeks. I was with my brother at the London hospital when the doctors told us that Reda would not survive and that perhaps switching off the life-support machine would be the best option.

Miraculously, Reda did wake up, but there was a long and arduous recovery journey in front of him.

Back in Ghana I'd managed, with the help of a friend of mine who knew the bank's CEO, to negotiate to replace the hostile young executive in charge of my account with a more senior one. Despite the change in account managers, the bank did want a shorter-term repayment plan. That meant we had to lean on suppliers, implement some cost-cutting measures to help with cashflow, and fire some employees. Though letting go of staff was unpleasant, I would've done anything to keep the company alive.

From a young age, I was blessed with an entrepreneurial spirit, no doubt inherited from my father. At sixteen, while still at college in the UK, I set up a small enterprise where I'd buy movies and television series on VHS tape to sell to several video clubs in Ghana. It was a good side business that earned me some extra cash to supplement the pocket money I already received from my father. I'd spend everything I earned going out, buying stuff, and living the "good life," as I had defined it then. That's when I first began striving for affluence. I wanted to make money so that I could spend it. I wanted to keep up with my friends, many from wealthy backgrounds, who could easily afford that lifestyle.

My father was a self-made man who'd transformed his life from extreme poverty in Lebanon to become richer than he ever dreamt he could be as an expat, first in Ghana and then in the U.K. However, by the time I reached my formative years in England, he was going through a hard time, and we were not as rich as the others in our circle. A theme that would visit me almost thirty-five years later.

I started my business in 1994 with a small sum of money I'd earned while working for my father's glass and mirror manufacturing business in Ghana. Aided by favourable rent terms and relying on my father's stellar reputation, I started to import building materials from Europe to cater to the ever-growing need for new homes in Ghana. Within a few years, I started to make good money and never looked back. However, without savings or a rich benefactor to support me, I had to succeed at all costs.

By September of 2007, I had steadied the ship at my company. On the surface, things looked good, but those five harrowing months had taken an immense toll. Unpleasant phone calls from bank representatives, threatening emails from suppliers, and the emotional turmoil of Reda's roller coaster recovery journey kept me in a constant state of stress and anxiety.

When the bank and suppliers stopped calling, I started to breathe easier, but I was always one missed sale, one mistake, or one disgruntled stakeholder away from disaster. There was a lot of pressure on me. The company was what sustained my lavish lifestyle and all the things I'd dreamt of. I had to make it work.

One night, I dreamt that I was being chased by three suited men while I ran, head down, carrying several heavy bags, one on my back and a smaller one across my chest, only to reach sand at the edge of the sea. Ahead, in the middle of the ocean, Reda lay on a hospital bed surrounded by doctors, his parents, and IV tubes, but he still had his angelic smile. I didn't know whether to swim into the ocean or turn around to face the three men. Perhaps the dream foreshadowed the self-discovery journey that I'd take. Either way, it became clear that I had to choose between continuing the "striving life" as depicted by the men in suits or discovering my authentic self, the one Reda offered me there in the sea.

The rainy season in Ghana was coming to an end that September day in 2007. Big raindrops splashed against my office window. The phone rang. It was one of my sales reps, calling to inform me that we had just lost a bid we couldn't afford to lose.

"Just give me the bottom line," I yelled into the phone. "Is it the price? Or do they want a specific brand we don't have?"

He mumbled something inaudible.

Before he could say anything else, I hurled the phone against the white wall in front of me. It shattered into many tiny pieces. Meanwhile, I collapsed down onto the leather office chair. I was short of breath, and my heart was beating at rocket speed. My right hand shook as I gasped for air. I thought that I was having a heart attack.

I took a few deep breaths and walked to the bathroom, splashing cold water on my face. The mirror reflected an image of a ghost—white skin, cold sweat beads all over my face and a bald head. I returned to my office, drank a glass of water, and sat for a few minutes until my breathing normalised.

That lost sale meant I couldn't pay the bank what I owed them that month. My heart sank as I thought of a repeat of what I'd been through already. Thankfully, a few weeks later, we somehow made a different sale just before month's end that nearly covered the dues for the bank.

Even though I'd bought us a reprieve and I was breathing easier, I knew I was in trouble. I had led the turnaround through shouting, intimidation, and bullying. I was like a stray cat who'd gone too many days without food, without reflection, without reason. Both at home and at work, my mood swings were becoming more apparent with every passing day. I was always angry, frustrated, and worried. I would vent my anger on whoever was closest to me—my wife, my employees, my kids, the waiter in a restaurant, or the driver who dared to cut me off.

Later that month, on a Sunday morning while driving to our riverside retreat with the family, I was stopped by the traffic police, who randomly stop drivers, especially in expensive-looking cars, trying to solicit bribes.

"Can I have a look at your papers," the young police officer standing outside my window said with a grimace on his face. I calmly got them out, perfectly in order, and showed them to the officer.

"No, these aren't the right ones. Please come down and report to my senior," he said.

I was getting agitated. "My papers are in order. I pass here every week, and you stop me every week," I said.

"You can't address a police officer that way," he replied. "Please come down to the station."

My face reddened. "All you want to do is to aggravate me and collect a bribe."

Offended, he started yelling at me, his rifle hanging on his shoulder, demanding I come out. I did so and was quickly surrounded by a few other officers who were now all shouting at me. I lost my head completely and started screaming back, telling them that they had no right to keep doing this week in, week out. Our faces inches apart, we both spewed angry words furiously at each other.

As I turned back to the car, I saw my daughter's face was white with terror.

I then heard my son's quiet voice from the window say, "Please, Dad, stop screaming."

His words hit me like a cold shower. I stopped.

A friend who had pulled up just behind me eventually sorted matters out, no doubt with much money being exchanged. I was grateful, but the image of my daughter and my son's words would haunt me for days.

On my arrival to our chalet, with my wife busy with preparations for the guests and my children in the water, I found a quiet area to light up a cigar before my friends arrived. I was desperate for some calm, but it didn't last long. Within minutes, guests started pulling in the drive.

The retreat was meant to be a place where I went to relax with friends, family, and all of our children. My wife and I would host our group of friends every other weekend. From the outside, our time there looked perfect. But the truth was that I wasn't enjoying my down time. Instead, I felt obligated to serve and pretend that everything was just fine.

Throughout my ordeal, I kept a brave face and never uttered a word of my woes to anyone. I would not allow myself to be vulnerable. I had to be perfect in the eyes of everyone and especially my family and friends. The retreat had become a place of burden instead of a place to relax. Unbeknownst to me, I'd developed such resentment for it that after my kids left for college, I quickly sold it and never set foot in the area again.

After everyone left, we had to pack up and lock up, a process that took over an hour. My mind was now on my impending travel to China within the next few days. I was going to visit the famous Canton fair. One of our company's guiding principles was to buy European and not Chinese. That was one of the reasons for our success. However, it was a new dawn in world trade as Chinese factories and their agents were undercutting prices and matching quality from Europe. Goods we bought from Italy and Spain were now being produced in abundance and at almost half the price. We couldn't miss out on such an opportunity. At the end of the day, the customers wanted quality and our assurance of that quality.

On the way back to Ghana, the plane hit some strong turbulence. It wasn't something atypical, yet I started shivering, overcome by a cold sweat and anxiety. This was the same turbulence I had felt many times before, yet the fear in me was something new. I was sure the plane would crash. I tightened the seat belt, got into a brace position, and pleaded with God to spare my life. This lasted for about ten minutes, and Joe, sitting next to me couldn't hide his surprise. But to me, the fear was visceral and real, and that incident ignited a fear of flying that remained with me for several years afterwards.

The silliest things now made me anxious–things that had never impacted me before, like going to parties, attending social gatherings, or holding business meetings with suppliers or customers. Being CEO of my company and socially active in our community meant that I couldn't stop doing these things even though I was a nervous wreck. But what made everything worse in this period of my life was that, in stark contrast to those around me, I wasn't happy. I felt an emptiness that I'd never felt before.

One night toward the end of November, my wife and I were invited to a dinner party, and I didn't want to go. Frowning at my wife, I said, "I prefer we skip tonight."

"We went to Amy's party last weekend. It won't be nice if we don't go to Judy's tonight. You know about their rivalry," she said, smiling.

I was stuck in a never-ending, vicious cycle. Being part of this high society group had a price. It meant I couldn't just decide not to do certain things even if I didn't feel up to it.

That night, I swallowed my feelings, got dressed, and went to get my Rolex watch from the small safe in our bedroom. I had a choice of three Rolexes which I had bought over the last few years, yet I felt that none of them was right. I wanted something to match my sky-blue linen shirt. I tried the silver one, but it didn't look good. Finally, I left for the party without a watch, feeling angry and frustrated, with no idea how entitled and privileged I'd become.

At the party, I drank heavily, something I'd started to do more often at parties "so that everyone would be more interesting," I would tell everyone. I'd heard that was what Hemingway said when asked about his over-drinking.

The next morning, I woke up with a headache and a sore throat but drove to the Rolex shop to order the Deepsea Sea-Dweller Rolex with a dark blue watch face. I paid but left the shop without the feel-good factor I usually got when buying something nice. Instead, it felt like a duty.

I was slowly changing. What used to make me happy no longer seemed to work. Now the stuff I bought didn't lift me. Instead, I felt nothing. Were these the first signs of my growing self-awareness?

Christmas arrived and I finally felt some excitement as our winter holiday approached. We were taking the kids to meet up with my brother, his family, and another couple in St. Moritz, the famous Swiss ski resort, where all the rich and famous went. We flew into Geneva and planned to drive up to the Alps a few days before New Year's Eve. We had to wait a long time before the car rental agency gave us our car. Instead of what I'd reserved, I was given a small Fiat Uno, which could barely fit our luggage let alone the kids. Of course, I had a long argument with the rep before letting up and accepting there was nothing I could do. I was now both tired and livid.

I was sweating now even though it was freezing outside. "Why do we have to travel with so much luggage," I screamed at my wife. I started to breathe heavily again and just couldn't calm myself down. I threw the bags into the boot and slammed it with so much force that it bounded back open. There was no way the bags would fit, and I was so furious that I became a spectacle to both my family and those in the car park.

Finally, I allowed my wife to help, and she suggested we put two of the bags in the backseats. The kids could then squish onto one backseat and lean onto the window. We drove in total silence for the next few hours until the majestic scenery outside calmed my mood.

On our arrival at the hotel, we were handed a welcoming glass of champagne. The resort was stunning, situated in the Engadin valley and surrounded by the Alps. All the people there were as beautiful and rich as you'd expect in St. Moritz. I quickly forgot all about my overreaction at the car rental pick up place. For a few days, I even forgot about all the woes I'd faced in the past months. I was happy that my kids were learning and enjoying how to ski and snowboard. The smiles on their faces reinforced the lessons my father taught me: work hard, make money, take care of my family, climb the status ladder, and enjoy the fruits.

Still, most of the time I found myself feeling like an imposter. I didn't deserve this glamour and lifestyle. Questions lingered at the back of my mind about whether I could actually afford these lavish trips or whether I was truly being myself in this environment of wealth and prestige.

Back in Ghana in April of 2008, I was watching television with the kids when I felt an acute pain in my chest. Just like that, I fell out of my chair and let out a scream. The chest pains were more intense than they'd ever been before, and they continued all night. Certain that I'd just had a heart attack, I called a doctor just past midnight. He came over and checked me out, saying that all my vitals were good. It had nothing to do with my heart. Perhaps it was something gastrointestinal. I had, after all, eaten badly the day before. He asked me to stop by his clinic on Monday for further tests but said there was nothing to worry about.

Even so, I was scared. There had been too many hairy moments in the last year or so. There must be something wrong with me. I recalled my ghost-like face in the mirror when I screamed at the sales rep, my minutes of madness and the look of terror on my daughter's face with the police. I could not control my emotions or the reaction of my body. Perhaps my body was telling me that enough was enough and that I had to change. I couldn't go on like a sleeping volcano waiting for an excuse to explode.

I didn't go to the clinic that Monday. Instead, I booked an appointment in faraway Lebanon. Though I'd never lived in Lebanon, I always found myself returning there for the big things like funerals, weddings, and medical emergencies, and it was there that my wife gave to birth to both our children.

A week later, I was on a plane heading to Lebanon to see a renowned heart specialist. May, the start of spring, always brought Lebanon's best weather, so I decided to also treat this as a short holiday, away from all the pressure and stress that I'd gone through over the past few months. I was eager to find the cause of these sudden heart throbbing incidents that I was having and wanted the reassurance from a top doctor that there was nothing wrong with me. Also, I was yearning for peace, quiet, and some downtime sprinkled with great Lebanese food, sunsets, and the sea.

When I landed in Beirut, the sun was out, but the remnants of winter's chill lingered in the air. My parents were in England visiting Reda, so I was all alone. I decided to stay in the Movenpick Hotel by the sea. I checked in just in time for sunset and went outside on the balcony to watch the sun slowly descend into the turquoise Mediterranean Sea. The freshness in the air gave me a buzz, something I hadn't had for a long while. I lit a Habanos cigar and took a deep inhale. The cigar burned beautifully, like a meteor illuminating the sky. I puffed out the smoke, and my throat burned for a few seconds. The smoke rose with my restless thoughts, both evaporating into thin air.

The next day, after I'd spent hours undergoing all the requisite tests, the doctor summoned me in.

"There is nothing wrong with you physically. Your heart is fine, and all the blood tests were fine. You have a little Vitamin D shortage but nothing serious."

"What about my chest pains, shortness of breath, and all that anxiety?" I asked with raised eyebrows.

"Your problems have nothing to do with your heart but instead with your head."

I shook my head incredulously.

"I think you're having panic attacks. That's why I'm recommending you see a psychiatrist."

"A what?" I couldn't believe what he was saying. I of all people did not need to see a shrink. I'd been self-reliant since I was ten years old. I'd taken care of myself most of my life.

"Maybe all I needed was a short break to watch the sunset," I said to my wife, trying to explain that perhaps I needn't see a psychiatrist. I was back at the hotel, enjoying breakfast on the balcony.

"No! You're not going to ignore what happened the last time. I was really scared. Anyway, you are already in Lebanon, so what would an hour cost you?"

She was right of course, but I still wasn't comfortable with the idea of seeing a doctor of the mind.

"It won't be easy getting an appointment as the doctor told me she's always busy," I tried.

"Let me worry about that."

True to her word, my wife got me an immediate appointment through a friend of a friend. There was no hiding place now.

I was biting my nails, an old habit that has never gone away, when the receptionist asked me to go in.

After some small talk, the doctor got down to business. "Why are you here?" she asked rather sternly. "Describe your feelings in the last few months."

Feeling rather awkward, I mechanically explained to her about both Reda's accident and my company's woes.

"But how did you feel?" she asked.

"I was afraid and maybe a bit anxious of how things would unfold, but I never had any chest pains or attacks during those five months. It was only after."

"Trauma is stored in our bodies, and reactions often come only after the event passes."

My face tightened. "I'd be fine, but then some petty incident drives me nuts. I become an enraged bull. When the rage subsides, I get the chest pains and have to sit or lie down."

I went on to explain the incident I had with the police officer and the phone call with the sales rep. "I'm still embarrassed of how my kids viewed me that day with the police officer."

"Explain to me how you felt at the onset of these attacks."

I told her about the shortness of breath, the pain in my chest, and my pounding heart.

She nodded. "These are the exact symptoms of a panic attack. It's your body telling you that it needs some rest."

Surely, the best doctors in Lebanon must be right. It was as she said. My body was reacting after trauma. However, I was still not entirely convinced.

"How do you feel when you're doing things you enjoy? Dinner with friends or spending time with your kids."

Now feeling more comfortable, I paused and thought. It was true that even with people whom I considered my inner circle, I had felt indifferent recently.

"I don't know; maybe I'm not being me. I've been rather restless, wanting everything I start to finish quickly, even if it's a dinner with friends, which I used to enjoy. It's as if I am just passing the time, logging in when I wake up and logging out when I'm going to bed."

After some more questions, she finally scribbled away for some minutes and looked up at me with a smile. "Don't worry. Your case is quite normal.

Many men like you at middle age and with heavy responsibilities go through what you are feeling now."

I remained silent.

"You see, a panic attack is a heightened state of anxiety when your body starts giving you warnings that it can no longer cope."

Now she was making more sense. I'd been through a lot, and I wasn't a twenty-something anymore.

"Okay, but what next?" I asked, becoming impatient with the repeated diagnosis.

"I think you need to go on a medication programme to help calm your frayed nerves and to put you in a better mood. I will prescribe Xanax, anti-anxiety tablets, for six months and Zoloft, an anti-depressant, for two years. Their combined effect will help you calm down and will ease the pressure on you so that you can be yourself again."

"What? Pills! Two years? It seems a bit too much."

"The two-year period is necessary so that your feelings are regulated, and you don't fall into a full-blown depression that panic attacks could lead to."

I was more than a little sceptical. "Let me think about this."

Ignoring what I said, the doctor stood up and handed me a prescription. "You can come and see me or call me in two weeks' time—but only after taking the pills."

"What about any side effects of the tablets?"

"There could be a few. At the beginning, there could be some nausea and loss of appetite, and then you might lose a few kilos. It's nothing major, but if you feel that there are major side effects, then please stop taking the pills immediately and call me."

I nodded silently, took the prescription, and left. Immediately on leaving her office, I called my sister, a psychologist, who confirmed what the doctor had said, adding that I follow the doctor's strict instructions on how to take them. And, more importantly, if I did start on them, I couldn't just casually stop them. I had to follow the doctor's instructions.

I stopped at the pharmacy with the prescription in hand and bought the drugs. I would only take them once I was fully convinced, I told myself.

I went back to my hotel balcony to watch the sunset again with a cigar in hand, what was fast becoming a daily sacred ritual. I pondered the doctor's questions and why an acclaimed doctor in her field thought I needed meds.

The sun descended into the sea and was nearly gobbled up by it. Within a few minutes it disappeared into the watery vastness. I was hypnotised by the sight. Coupled with the effect of the cigar and a short glass of cognac, I went into a more profound and emotional world, and my eyes teared up. I felt lost and confused.

I'd done everything correctly within the formula of success I had learned, yet I hadn't been happy, even before this turbulent year. Worse still, all my friends and family who followed the same formula seemed happy. Everything felt like a race, as if I were running toward an endless goal. I would be buoyed by achieving a certain milestone only to feel down when I failed. Sometimes I felt even worse when I achieved my objective. I wanted everything to finish quickly and never enjoyed the actual thing that I was doing at the time. I had no appreciation of the present moment and never felt the rush of flow I'd find much later in my life.

The traumatic events of the previous year seemed to have impacted me more than I had initially thought. I'd never felt more vulnerable or afraid. It was like I was being attacked from all angles. It was the first time that I had paused to think and to reflect on whether what I was doing was right.

Perhaps now more than ever, I needed some support. Yes, I'd take the pills. I was tired of feeling empty. I was tired of feeling rushed with everything I did. I wanted to enjoy the holidays, the riverside retreat, and being around my friends and family. I knew something needed to change.

Chapter 2

In Times of War, I Found My Peace

Still in my hotel room in Lebanon, I took the first dose of the medication and intended to nap, only to become fascinated by the local news. There were rising tensions between two sect-dominated political groups, one backed by the Sunni Muslims and the pro-western government, the other by Shia Muslims.

Put simply, Lebanon is a country that is always at war. The country is divided into many different religions, sects, and factions, which means, even when at peace, there is often ongoing political conflict, just without the guns. Every time unity is found, somehow a new schism disrupts the peace. Power has changed hands many times over the years. First the Christians took power, then the Sunni Muslims took over after the civil war. Now, to my father's delight, the Shia Muslims, who represent a large percentage of the population, were attempting to take over.

My father was born and brought up in a small historical town called Tyre, which was predominantly Shia. His pious father adhered strictly to the edicts of Islam. Their family was large, and they were very poor. Both my father and uncle had to work from an early age. During my father's early years, the Shias were mostly uneducated and had little power in Lebanon. He and most Shias felt victimised and inferior to the Sunnis and Christians. That's why many Shias support Hezbollah to this day and look past the "Party of God's" indiscretions because they at least put the Shias on the Lebanese map.

Due to their many wars, whether between factions or against invading neighbouring states, the Lebanese have learned to take the tensions and reports in stride and continue to live normally until a full-blown war breaks out. However, the country was rife with rumours that a face-off was coming in the next few weeks.

An hour after taking the pills, as I lay there still watching the news, I began having stomach cramps and felt queasy. As the darkness outside began to seep into the room, I started to feel something I'd never felt before. It was as if I were alone in this world, surrounded by nothingness. I remained in bed but was overtaken by a wave of despair. My heartbeat quickened, my mouth dried up, and I just couldn't rid myself of this terrible feeling. Not only did I have to endure the physical side effects of these pills, but I also felt ashamed that I had to take meds to help get me back on track. It was as if a war were ready to erupt inside of me just as it was outside my hotel's walls.

I took a cold shower, lay in bed, and soon drifted into a deep sleep only to be awakened by the television that I had inadvertently left on. Feeling better, I drank a glass of water and slept again. After sleeping for about fourteen hours, I woke a second time when the emanating warmth of the sun entered my room. Though I felt groggy and heavy at first, as if I had a hangover, the sunlight quickly brightened my mood. I then had breakfast in bed and took my second dose. Though I feared the worst, this time around the symptoms were milder, but my mood was still blue.

In the evening I met up with a family friend, Mark, who was staying at the same hotel I was along with two of his friends. Again, the conversation was dominated by one topic—the unfolding political crisis. They were all very agitated and anxious about what was going to happen in the upcoming few days. The media were apocalyptic, inciting both the leaders of the different sects and the Lebanese people. Each television station blamed the leader they didn't support and gave differing opinions, scenarios, and expectations. If ever one could demonstrate confirmation bias at its worst, then the different television stations did so.

Unlike Mark and his friends, I didn't feel any apprehension. I'd never lived in Lebanon and didn't have much at stake. True, I had some sympathy for the Shia plight because of my father and the stories he'd told me regarding the oppression he and many Shias went through in the past. But I hadn't felt any of it myself. As a third culture kid—born and raised in Ghana, living my formative years in England, and carrying the traditions of my Lebanese parents—I had no country that felt like home.

I left them talking and decided to walk back to the hotel. The normally loud streets of Beirut were eerily quiet. Just before I turned right onto the main street leading to the hotel, I met a road blockade.

"Where are you going? I need your ID," said a young army officer.

The uniform, the rifles, and the checkpoint brought back my anxiety from the last confrontation I had with the police in Ghana. My lips trembled, and my heart rate increased. I showed him my ID and pointed to where my hotel was. He waved me through with an uneasy look in his eyes.

What if a war did break out? Back in my room, I again took my medication. The side effects I'd had on the first day were all but gone, so I quickly fell into a deep sleep.

"Dhak. Dhak. Dhak. Dhak."

A loud noise woke me up. At first, I wasn't sure what it was, thinking it was either thunder or that I had left the television on. It was non-stop—the rattling sound of gunfire that I had heard in many movies.

I got up and went to the balcony, and now the noise was unmistakable. With my heart beating much faster, I could see the light and fire emanating from the top of a tall apartment building to my left. I focused more on the glare. A large kind of artillery, like a big machine gun on a tripod, fired shot after shot, leaving a trail of fire on the skyline. There was a lot of activity close to our hotel—men running in the streets, setting up roadblocks, and burning tires as if to mark their territories. The scene was surreal, like from a war movie.

I fumbled my way toward the far end of the balcony only to retreat to the bed as the hotel room's phone rang. It was Mark.

"It's happening. Come up to my room. It's 679 on the sixth floor," he said.

With clammy hands and an urgent step, I hurried to his room. His door was open. The view from his balcony was even better than mine. Now we could see two groups of men firing at each other.

We went to the lobby, which faced the main road but on a level below the street. Outside, military tanks were now on the move, and we glimpsed several men running about wearing all-black uniforms and holding AK-47 rifles. Our hotel seemed to be at the centre of the fighting, and we would later learn that it was only five hundred yards away from where the fiercest battles took place.

"Please go back to your rooms," the deputy hotel manager said.

Mark's eyes were filled with terror. Only now did it dawn on me that I was in danger. It didn't help that Mark was now getting updates from his friends, who alerted him that there was a mini war being fought near our hotel on an avenue that separated Hezbollah-backed Shiite and future Sunni areas, a battle that quickly spread out to other parts of Beirut. Both sides were using machine guns and rocket-propelled grenades.

Around 4:00 a.m., the gunfire subsided, and I went to my room exhausted. I slept until Mark woke me up the next day. He'd come to tell me the bad news—the airport was closed indefinitely. Knowing there was no easy exit was like a punch in the face. I felt helpless and lost. On the one hand, I was happy that my parents were in England, visiting Reda. Having no close family around meant I only had to worry about myself. On the other hand, I was completely alone, cut off from all family and with only Mark to rely on.

As soon as the news was out in the world, I started getting calls from family and friends. Everyone had some advice on what to do and not to do.

My father called to give me the contact information of someone he knew who could help if matters worsened.

I felt sure things would be resolved in the next couple of days. The full story was unfolding: most of the battles had ended, and some were still raging on. The bottom line was that the Hezbollah-led Shia group had taken over the city and crushed their opposition quickly.

By late afternoon, things had calmed down, and the Lebanese army—the only neutral entity in Lebanon, trusted by everyone—had taken control. Mark and I were getting restless and decided to venture outside. We walked to Cafe Verdun, which was only a few minutes' walk from our hotel. The streets were like a battleground—road barriers erected to cordon off areas, military tanks, and army personnel everywhere, all with AK-47s on their shoulders.

"Where are you going?" said an army officer as we passed him.

"To Cafe Verdun. We have been in the hotel for a long time and just wanted to get outside," said Mark.

Typically, even the Lebanese army is not strict. They understood our need to get out and about. We showed our IDs, and he waved us on.

We didn't see any burned buildings or any people lying dead on the street as some of the media were asserting. It seemed that the battle was precise and in a few specific areas.

We arrived at the usually buzzing café and found it empty but for the screams of three men sitting by the window—Mark's friends, of course. All three were talking at each other and barely noticed us when we sat down. There was much gesticulating and finger wagging. Best friends of yesterday were today quarrelling on opposite sides, and everyone had his own version of events.

"I'd always respected Hezbollah and Sayyad Hassan—but not anymore. Turning their guns on the Lebanese is not acceptable," Rami said.

"It was self-defence. What do you expect them to do? Sit and watch while the American-backed government dismantles their defence system?" Ali said.

More uproar followed. Mark tried to calm them down.

The third man stood up to leave. "I'm not going to sit and argue about this. Hezbollah have killed Sunnis tonight."

"But Shias were also killed by Sunnis. It was the Sunnis who attacked first," said Ali.

Both Rami and the other man stood up now, screaming their heads off. They left our table and headed out.

I sat calmly and listened to all the arguments. I was trying to make sense of the politics and be as objective as I could, but it wasn't easy with Mark around. He was a staunch Hezbollah and Shia sympathiser.

Even though I was far away from home and from my family—and in a war zone—rather surprisingly, I wasn't scared. My heart was not beating fast like it had a few days ago when the army officer stopped me at the checkpoint or when I screamed at my sales rep. The reality was that I was intrigued by the excitement of it all, something different to the mundanity of my life back home. With the meds numbing my fearful thoughts, it all felt like an adventure. Most importantly, there were no expectations on my shoulders or any responsibilities to anyone. I had no decisions to make on an hourly basis, unlike back home.

I spent the next few days in this routine: hotel, lunch and listening to the arguments, back to the hotel, dinner and more arguing. All the places we went to were within walking distance, and we discussed only one topic. No other conversation had a chance. The calls from family and friends also kept coming. Seen through the eyes of the media far away from Beirut streets, everyone thought it was far more dangerous than it was.

"Dad, are you safe? When are you coming back home?" my twelve-year-old son asked on one of the phone calls.

"I'm waiting for the airport to open. Then I'll be back home. I'm good and having fun, so don't worry," I reassured him.

"But what if it doesn't open for a while? My friend at school told me that there will be more fighting. Find a way to come back. Please."

I promised that I would. His words found a way to wake me from my stupor. Perhaps the pills had quelled my anxiety to such an extent that I was ambivalent about the reality of Lebanon's never-ending conflicts. Perhaps it was now time to share Mark's eagerness to leave. Since the airport was closed, we had only two options: by road through Syria, which was long and arduous, or across the Mediterranean Sea to Cyprus.

Through the hotel concierge, Mark and I arranged to meet a supposed sea captain who would explain how he could take us across the Mediterranean.

"Hello, I'm Antoun," he said. He was dressed in '70s clothes, had a fake cigar in his mouth, and could easily be mistaken for a member of the Sicilian mafia with his thick black hair and a thicker moustache.

He showed us a picture of what looked more like a ski boat not suitable for making an eight-hour sea journey.

"Can this small boat really navigate the waters?" I asked.

Antoun got up to leave, agitated by my question. "Of course, it can. I've done this hundreds of times. Who do you think I am?"

Did he really expect us to risk our lives in that thing?

"How much would the trip be?" Mark asked.

"Ten thousand dollars," he said. Mark and I looked at each other in disbelief. We thanked him and quickly left. To risk our lives on such a journey was stupid and to pay such an amount was even more stupid. The Syria route was even more dangerous because you had to know the right people to navigate it and we didn't. Circumstances were not that dire yet.

Though things were calm around the hotel, there was also no denying that if we couldn't yet leave Lebanon, we needed to get away from this part of Beirut. Things could quickly spiral out of control if history was anything to go by. The next morning, on Mark's advice, we packed our bags and left together to head to Jounieh, a town in the Christian sector of Lebanon.

We got there at noon. The roads were empty though crammed with many army checkpoints. We checked into a hotel, and it was as if we had moved to another country. Jounieh had the usual hustle and bustle of Beirut, but it was much smaller. Most noticeably, they were oblivious to what was happening less than one hour and twenty-three kilometres away.

We spent the next few days there. Our routine was straightforward: breakfast, coffee, lunch, coffee, dinner, and then finally a bar, all with the same friends from Beirut who had now also moved there. We punctuated our nights by watching long political speeches while I daydreamed of how I could take this surprising inner peace I felt back home with me. How could I slow down and stop my constant running around? How could I live an anxiety-free life?

I was so entrenched in the present—the daily political updates, which road was closed, and the rumours flying around about some of the leaders—that I was far removed from the anxiety and depression I felt back home. I would learn later that living in the present and not replaying the past or planning for the future is one of the pillars of living a contented life.

The anti-depressants were doing their work in that my feelings were frozen, at least temporarily, which was a far cry from the emotional roller coaster I had been on before arriving in Lebanon. I didn't feel much joy, but there was also no anxiety or any depression. I wasn't smiling or laughing much, but I wasn't frustrated or angry. Most importantly, there were no sharp pains to the heart, which I now understood to be panic attacks. I was satisfied that the drugs were working and that they had calmed me down enough so that I could think objectively and become more serene.

The truth was that I was feeling peaceful in a time of war.

I liked the fact that I could just sit and listen and that no one expected me to say anything. I enjoyed being led by Mark rather than having the burden always fall to me to make daily decisions. I relished the uncertainty of my day-to-day life and wasn't in a hurry to get back home to the usual mundanity. I found myself retreating from my reactive mind and being more reflective on my life. I was now more relaxed than I had been for a long time and asking myself the big questions again.

Naturally, being in Lebanon made me think of my father and how his upbringing must have shaped his values and actions. At age sixteen, against the odds, he'd become a rising star working for the town's richest trader and making them a lot of money. At eighteen, he was offered a job to go and work in lucrative Africa. He married my mother, who was then sixteen, and they moved to a new and distant country. My father was hungry, fearless, enterprising, and wanted to prove himself. He was also deeply faithful, which gave him a strong surety and trust in life. He could recite wholeheartedly any verse from the Koran.

It was a complete contrast to how I was brought up. I was comfortable, fearful, and based my beliefs on evidence, not religion. Looking back, it was little wonder that the magic formula that worked for him would not work for me.

One morning, I went for a walk alone near the city centre. Inadvertently, I ended up in the tattoo shop. All kinds of pictures were plastered on its walls—pictures of tattooed people, cool dragon sketches, paintings and pictures of graffiti along some street walls of Beirut. Deep Purple played loudly in the background, and a short boyish man with tattoo-covered arms looked up at me.

"What do you want to do? I'm free for the next hour. After that, it will have to be next Thursday," he said.

"Oh no. I'm just looking around," I said. I had never wanted a tattoo, yet my interest was piqued.

"Okay sure, but I'm quite busy—and customers will start walking in any minute now," he said.

"What would a winged angel with the words 'born to be free' look like?" I asked. The image had just popped into my head. To this day, I have no reasonable explanation for how the tattoo came about.

He drew it freehand on tracing paper, showed it to me, and said, "C'mon, get in the chair."

Inexplicably, I did. After a few hours of listening to all the rock music from the '80s, I came out with a massive tattoo on my right shoulder. I looked in the mirror, the tattooist smiling behind me. It was beautiful. He was a true artist.

Sometimes we do things without knowing why or before we know why. Perhaps my inner self was always screaming for freedom, and I had only heard the message when my mind quieted in the noisiest of situations. The tattoo was an image that encapsulated how I was feeling. All I wanted was to free myself from all the burdens, responsibilities, and baggage that I'd been carrying for so long. Most of all, I wanted to free myself from my father's most foundational Lebanese value—the thirst to strive.

Fresh from getting a tattoo and feeling the after-effects—a swelling and slight burning sensation on my shoulder—I walked into a bookshop called Antoine. I browsed the aisles of books. Many were in French, and a lot were about the Lebanon wars. I found an English section that contained some famous literary texts. Charles Dickens, Shakespeare's sonnets, and Melville's *Moby Dick* all lay in front of my eyes, but I was drawn to Leo Tolstoy's *The Death of Ivan Illich*. I bought it and walked back to the hotel. Mark had gone to meet some friends, and I told him I'd catch up with him at dinnertime. I ordered coffee and started to read immediately.

By evening, I was almost halfway through and just couldn't put it down. The protagonist, Ivan, a middle-aged lawyer who lived a life of mediocrity, devoid of many emotions and busy trying to earn the esteem of the people in his circle, is struck by a sudden illness. He lies down dying and reflects on his mortality. Like those around him, he had always considered death as something that happened to others. Now, for the first time, he becomes conscious.

Had he lived his life wrongly or as others expected him to? Had he lived for the so-called benefits that society brings—honour, wealth, and a modicum of pleasure? Why had he failed to realise that this was his life, one that he must self-author?

As his death beckons, Ivan becomes more content, realising that his previous barely perceptible attempt to rebel against his artificial and superficial life (and those around him) was, in fact, the true way of living—to live with more meaning. He then smiles and dies.

Ivan's final thoughts had a tremendous effect on me, and I asked myself that simple question: "What if I was living my life all wrong?" What if living authentically didn't mean worrying about what people thought of my life or what I thought was right under my conditioned beliefs but, instead, what my heart thought was true.

After a few more days in Jounieh, we got the call from someone high up—of course one of Mark's friends—that it had finally calmed down in Beirut and that the big external countries (Saudi Arabia, Iran, France, and the USA) had interfered as always to prop up the two sparring factions. A peace summit would be held in Doha, Qatar, and, almost twelve days since its closing, the airport was to be reopened within the next few days.

Mark and I said our goodbyes, and I went back to the hotel in Beirut where I had first stayed, leaving him behind in Jounieh. He wanted to stay in Lebanon now that the partying had restarted. All the anxiety he had had suddenly disappeared when there was a good time on the horizon.

I wanted to go back to the normalcy of my life—my home, family, work, and friends. I felt stronger, calm enough to face all the responsibilities and decisions waiting for me.

On my last night, I sat on the balcony once again. This time, there was a lovely full moon, and I was facing a striking breeze. The moon shone brightly, reflecting its light on the mirror-like deep blue waters of the sea. It was a surreal moment, one that many poets and authors have spent hours detailing. It felt like a gift from the gods, as if they were sending me back home with an insight on what profound grace could look like. Without warning, tears started rolling down my cheeks. I didn't know why but it felt good, almost purifying, to cry.

I was overcome by conflicting feelings—a deep sense of shame over needing the anti-depressants and the knowledge that it was okay to give myself a break. It was okay for me to be vulnerable for once. It was okay to receive help through medication.

I felt Ivan Illich's plight viscerally as if we were one and the same and as if Tolstoy were describing my life under different circumstances. I wanted to change the direction of my life, to discover the real authentic me. I had to find a way to reconcile the two warring factions within me. Just like Lebanon's war divided the Sunnis and Shias, my own internal warring sides had me striving under the success formula that I'd inherited on one side and a new search for inner peace on the other. Somehow, I knew that peace would only come, much later, with a simpler and less materialistic life.

I looked at the full moon and made a promise to myself. I was grateful for how the pills regulated my nerves, but I would kick the anti-depressants out of my life within six months and endeavour to unravel the true authentic me without them.

I had run away from the turmoil and incessant pressure of the ordinariness of my life only to find my peace in the extraordinariness of war. I knew from that moment on that I had to shift my way of being. I had to find a new formula that could free the true me from the old me. I had to allow my inner voice the full freedom of expression that it was seeking. And most importantly, I now had the desire to find who the real me was—I wanted to change.

Chapter 3

In Search of the Miraculous

I returned from my Lebanon adventure knowing that I had to change, so I started my internal revolution. I read, watched, and listened to all kinds of teachings, philosophies, and ideas. I quickly chanced on a book, *Socrates Cafe: A Fresh Taste of Philosophy* by Christopher Phillips, in which Phillips revives the love of questions that Socrates inspired long ago in Greek philosophy. Phillips would set up meetings at coffee shops, libraries, schools, and churches during which groups of people reflected on the meaning of love, purpose, friendship, work, growing old, and life's other big questions. I was inspired by Phillips's book to create a group on Facebook that I called "Socrates Cafe," mirroring Phillips's ideas. Many of my friends joined to reflect on questions, including Ella, a good friend who volunteered to help with the administration of the group.

One day I posted, "How do we live a life of meaning?" This question had become central to my thinking. Work was stressful, monotonous, and joyless. I wanted to live a richer life but didn't know where to start. I was lost and confused, especially about how I could best live a purposeful life.

On the forum, the usual answers came in—taking care of family, earning money to feed and educate our children—but for me that wasn't enough. I wanted a specific and meaningful purpose that would challenge me. Perhaps the biggest obstacle to the change I sought was my own unreasonable expectations.

To me, finding one's purpose and living by it is why we are on Earth. However, I also knew from myself and everyone around me that to find and live by such a purpose was nothing short of miraculous.

Over the first six months after my trip to Lebanon, I was able to focus on my company and improve its performance. Finally, it was back in a good place, but internally I wasn't feeling much better. Instead, I became a robot without feelings. While raising my lows from the days of the panic attacks, the meds had also reduced my highs. The pills had served their purpose, but I needed to stop them. They had helped treat the symptoms, but the deeper underlying problem—dissatisfaction with my life—remained. This required me to do much internal work, and there was nothing the meds could do to help me there. I didn't know it then but finding that meaning and purpose would be a long and arduous journey. Getting off the pills was just the first step.

In the summer of 2009, a year after I'd started taking the pills, I followed the strict procedure recommended by the psychiatrist and weaned myself off them. The first few days were tough. On one gloomy afternoon, I felt so low that I was tempted to go back to the meds, something the doctor warned me about. Luckily, it passed, and the following weeks went smoothly. I was completely off the meds after four weeks.

Though it was a huge victory internally, I never shared it with anyone on the outside. Vulnerability at that time was something I frowned upon. I didn't yet understand it, nor had I experienced its power.

Meanwhile, I was active in the virtual cafe, which offered little clarity on my larger purpose but nevertheless ignited in me the love of asking questions, reflecting on answers, and going back out again for more and better questions—a refining process. It opened a Pandora's box within me, as all my intellectual curiosity had been locked up for so many years. Now, knowledge became the thread to grab onto while I was striving for meaning.

I quickly registered for many online courses, sometimes several in parallel, and bought up to five books each month. I read a vast variety of books that included memoirs, classic fiction, poetry, and philosophy. I was in a rush to digest every sentence ever written on how to live a good life. Looking for the quickest way to alleviate my dissatisfaction, I ended up using the same methodology to change myself as I did for making money. It was as if I were in a race and winning meant accumulation of courses and books.

What also made me more desperate to find meaning was the fact that I felt I had no right to be dissatisfied. My life was good; I was well-off financially, had a good business and a wonderful family, and was living a luxurious life. Perhaps I'd find that "loose screw" somewhere to regain my contentment, I told myself. All the information I consumed—books, podcasts, videos, and social media—pointed me toward the self-help industry. I genuinely thought that all my answers lay there. Looking back now, it was obvious that I'd replaced one addiction—chasing success, prestige, and money—with another: self-help teachings. My striving nervous system had kicked in again.

Over the next year or so, I kept reading more books, watching more documentaries, and studying TED Talks. I split my time between my company and my new passion for personal development. I was now less interested in our social scene and more focused on myself. The supposed extrovert was now turning inward.

My wife and kids were surprised at first but never made an issue out of this. Also significantly, some friends blindly backed me in every stage of my development. However, most around me were baffled by my new fascination. Though no one questioned me, I could feel the sniggering behind my back.

At work, my passion for my company dwindled as quickly as my interest in self-help grew. Often, I'd be conscious of not spending enough time running my company, but I just couldn't help myself. I was hellbent on finding more meaning in my life.

In November 2011, after following Bob Proctor online for a while, I received an email from Proctor's team announcing the "Matrixx" event, which promised all the strategies and tactics one needed to change within a week-long seminar. The email also stated that two places remained available. I had to confirm that day or lose my chance to meet Proctor. At that stage of my life, I saw Bob Proctor as the man who could save me. He was one of the leading teachers of how to change our mindset. I paid and reserved my seat.

I later realised this tactic is common in the self-help world—the gurus use an old marketing ploy by creating the fear of missing out. The dissatisfaction and lack of purpose in my life meant that I was only too eager to fall for it.

I travelled for almost eight hours, taking two flights to Toronto. On the first day of the event, the aging Bob Proctor ran into the large room to the sound of blazing music. He then launched into a forty-minute monologue. Being a talented and dramatic teacher, Proctor used the effects of lighting, music, and silence to teach his lessons. Most of us were transfixed during that time.

On the second day, Proctor introduced us to the "stick figure diagram" created by Dr. Thurman Fleet in the 1930s. He grabbed a marker and drew one big circle that he divided into two: the conscious mind at the top and the unconscious at the bottom. The circle signified our heads. He then connected it to a smaller ring, which represented our bodies, and drew its hands and legs, which signified our behaviours. The point was that our minds control our actions.

According to Fleet, we have two separate minds—the conscious and the unconscious. The conscious mind, which represents only five percent of our total brains, is the thinking mind, where we think freely and accept or reject any idea. It gets information from our five senses and is rooted in the present, e.g., when we hear a car approaching as we cross the road, we immediately stop.

The unconscious mind is like a supercomputer loaded with a database of programmed behaviours, most of which we acquire between birth and age six. This programming influences almost ninety-five percent of our thoughts, decisions, emotions, and actions. The unconscious is basically running our lives. Most of the time, we are unaware of our behaviours. For example, it becomes automatic to brush our teeth at night since we've done so for so many years. However, if not addressed quickly enough, our thoughts crystallise into core beliefs, which become almost impossible to shift.

How we understand a concept like money is totally dependent on how our parents thought, felt, and acted around it when we were young. My father was brought up poor and lived through hardships and scarcity. Considering his history, gaining financial security was his core belief, so his thirst for success, money, and a higher rung on the status ladder made sense. However, I was brought up differently; educated and with a more comfortable base. As such, the striving beliefs inadvertently passed down to me ultimately failed me.

Many of us know that our minds control our actions, yet few of us change them. Why do many of us fail miserably with our resolutions? Why are we stuck with behaviours we dislike? Our minds are the hardware, and our thoughts, beliefs, and paradigms are the software. Instead of trying to change the hardware, we should instead change the software, which are our thoughts and beliefs. If we create a habit of rising at 5:00 a.m. every day and get up without fail for the next three months, we magically become morning people who enjoy the sounds of the birds chirping, the wondrous silence, and the inner peace that brings to us. We have reprogrammed the supercomputer with new software.

I looked back at the last few traumatic years—before I had my panic attacks that led to the anti-depressants—with new eyes. I saw that the beliefs I grew up with had affected my every action. It made sense that I wanted to make money, buy a Rolex watch, and show my group that I'd made it. It was what had been modelled for me since I was a child, not only by my father but by every adult I came across, including family, friends we grew up with, and others from the wider Lebanese community living in Ghana. I knew no other world. That was my software.

I now understood that the ambivalence I felt years later was merely how my new way of thinking was fighting with the old way. The anxiety and the panic attacks were a message to me that I was going the wrong way against what I truly wanted. The anger and rage I felt was my frustration at not knowing what was wrong with me or what to do about it.

For me, the stick-figure diagram was an "a ha" moment. It was so simple yet effective. I could finally comprehend a tangible way to change. I couldn't simply think myself into change. Instead, I needed to address the thoughts, beliefs, and paradigms that lay dormant in my unconscious. But how?

"How can we reprogramme our subconscious? How can we make it change the thoughts it produces?" I asked Proctor.

"Repetition, my friend," he bellowed theatrically. "I want you to write out what you want in your journal every morning for the next thirty days."

He went on to explain that we need to auto-suggest to our subconscious mind what we want. It's a kind of self-hypnosis whereby we write out and then visualise the results we want daily. It's like the principle of "fake it till you make it." We trick our subconscious minds into believing that we already have what we were dreaming of.

The next day, Proctor talked about his involvement with the movie *The Secret*. In one of the scenes, a woman visualised a car. Within a few months, circumstances conspired so that a car arrived in her garage. Personally, I'd always found the scene somewhat phony and embarrassing. Now, Proctor was telling us that visualising something you wanted desperately meant you would get it. With this teaching, we started to enter the New Age world's spookiness and flakiness, and I wasn't impressed.

From creating a successful company, I knew first-hand that nothing manifests if you don't put in the work. Maybe visualisation does help put us in a positive state of mind, but nothing will magically appear without taking steps toward that goal. Olympic swimmers use visualisation techniques but also put in six hours of training every day.

Over the final few days, my frustrations grew further as I realised that the rest of the event focused on manifesting money in our lives.

"I need something more than money," I told Proctor when we had a private meeting.

"You're too comfortable. You need to up your game and aim for more money than you're earning," he said.

The last thing I wanted to hear was that I needed more money, especially not in such a sleazy manner. But he had hit a nerve by claiming I was too comfortable. I wanted to know why I was put on Earth. I was still naive enough to think that a purpose would appear magically to me. I knew how to make money, but I wanted satisfaction to go with it.

"Life is a game, and making money is one such way to live," Proctor continued.

"But I want my game to be bigger than money," I said to him. He smiled and turned away, saying nothing and leaving me confused.

On the last day, things got worse as Proctor encouraged us to enter multi-level marketing. MLMs are nothing but pyramid schemes for making money. I felt disappointed and disillusioned by his sleazy sales approach and his lust for money.

However, with my striver's thinking, I fell quickly for the marketing trap. The trick is to sign people up when they are high on adrenaline—and it worked. I ended up signing up for a year-long facilitator's programme. It was something I'd been debating in my mind throughout my week-long stay. Perhaps it was FOMO or the fact that I felt my involvement in a year-long programme would truly help my evolution.

Despite my disappointment, many of the principles Proctor taught us about our mindset and the stick-figure diagram were the genesis of my self-help journey. During the week-long stay in Toronto, it seemed easy to follow Proctor's instructions and be in that mindset of change. I'd get up early and write out my affirmations:

> "I, Mo, am a child of God. God wants me to be peaceful, powerful, and prosperous. I am a co-creator of my image. I must never waver in the faith that the universe is on my side and that whatever happens is in the

best interest of Mo. I'm responsible for my life, my thoughts, my feelings, my actions, my personal growth, and for every result I achieve. I now see myself as a person who is smiling. I'm peaceful, and it's seen on my face with positive energy flowing from me. I will be there for my children in a calm manner, helping them to make the right choices. I am very successful in my business. I am healthy and an example to all about how to eat and exercise. I am spiritually full and really understand the way of the universe and am ready to show it to others. I have purpose in my life and am loving every minute of life and hoping LIFE will never end."

It all felt natural in Toronto with like-minded people and the right environment around me. I was always in a positive state of mind, smiling as if I owned the world. But that all changed as soon as I got home. I'd learn later that this was a common occurrence among those who completed this type of workshop or seminar. We get elevated by the teachers, like-minded students, and the environment into a high-level state that can't be matched back home. What seemed inspirational and real only a few weeks ago looked woo-woo and unrealistic once we returned home.

Suddenly, when I added in my work responsibilities, family life, and social events, I didn't have enough time to do the affirmations, visioning exercises, or reading I had been doing in Toronto. Most of the people around me back home were not on the same wavelength, which made it hard to maintain my momentum. They'd find what I was saying hard to swallow or just irrelevant to real life. Some laughed in my face when I told them that I was writing out a paragraph from James Allen's book each morning for ten consecutive days and expecting it to change my mindset. Later, I'd also laugh at myself. I was, perhaps, taking the self-help practices too seriously.

Over the next few months, I did complete the course, but the Proctor team's promised support never materialised. Keeping in contact with the friends I made at the event also proved difficult. I developed a good friendship with two Australians, and we kept up our Skype calls for about a month until somehow life drowned us, and we stopped talking.

True, there were parts of the programme that I didn't like, but I had paid so much for it and had found the actual material good and truthful. So, I stuck to the programme and was certified to coach both in the corporate world and with individuals.

During the "Matrixx" event, I was captivated by the idea of playing a new game, as per Proctor's words, only this time one that was more meaningful. I wanted to set up a foundation that would help young, impoverished boys back home in Accra by educating them and training them in football. The fifty or so young boys I had in mind were from a poor part of Accra and regularly played football with my son and his friends. I would often help them by getting them gear or giving them some pocket money for the weekend. Setting up a foundation to help them more consistently seemed to be the next step in helping them have a better life.

The Born to be Free foundation was registered in late 2011, a few months after I came back from Toronto, and effectively launched in January of 2012. I named it after my tattoo and the symbol of my internal revolution. Somehow, I was trying to reclaim my own freedom through helping the kids claim theirs. Starting a foundation also seemed a wonderful way to imbue more meaning into my life.

Implementing the plan that I'd set up with the help of another coach I'd met in Toronto during Proctor's programme, I registered fifty boys aged ten to sixteen, enrolled them in schools, and arranged football sessions for them with a professional coach. I also started teaching life lessons, including the stick figure diagram, to the boys once a month. I was running the foundation on a part-time basis, one half day during the week and on Saturdays, while my full-time focus was still on my company.

The foundation did well at first, and I loved being involved with the boys, especially watching them train and play football. The intent was for the kids to sign professionally with bigger football clubs. That inspired them to practice hard and to go to school. However, to get them the training and exposure they'd need to go pro meant that I needed both financial help and a bigger team of people to help with running the day-to-day affairs. Most of my time was still preoccupied with my company, so I hired four more people to help with operations and to target donors. Expenses were piling up, and donations were not. Most people wanted to see that the foundation was operational for more than three years before they proffered any money.

When I stepped back from day-to-day management and hired an operations manager to run the foundation full time, I started to lose interest, a mistake I repeated in many aspects of my life. At first, I'd go all in in whatever project I was pursuing but then would slowly cool off. My impatience and lack of consistency and purpose would overcome my good intentions. That was part of the striver's disease, I'd learn later: looking for quick fixes and lacking the perseverance and the wherewithal to see things through in the long term.

I kept footing the bills for almost two years, but the foundation fizzled out. The football arena in Ghana is very competitive, and there were already football academies that were well-funded by European super clubs that specialised in rearing football talent. Football was also a world that was run by connections and knowing the right people. We didn't have any such connections, and, as a result, the chances of the BTBF kids making it as professionals were slim, if not impossible.

I was disheartened by my failure with the foundation. I'd thought that I had finally found something truly meaningful only to find out that, even though my heart was involved in the project, it still failed.

Without knowing it, I was now in search of the next new thing. I stumbled upon Neuro-Linguistic Programming, or NLP as it's better known. NLP is a self-empowerment system that is a cross between hypnosis, improved communication, and psychotherapy. It is meant to teach us skillsets that enable us to understand the language of our minds. In doing so, we can control our minds, change our behaviour, and understand others. It was developed by modelling great communicators and therapists. I thought it might be the quick fix that I craved, the mother of all systems through which I'd finally find a way to change completely and help others do the same.

In May 2012, I went to London for a seminar hosted by Richard Bandler, the co-creator of NLP. Bandler was funny, looked like a mix between Danny DeVito and Joe Pesci, and spoke like an Italian mobster, using expletives every other word. The NLP techniques we learned included concepts like dissociation, content reframing, anchoring, rapport, influence, and persuasion—big words that from the offset sounded difficult and remained so even after the training. No doubt the concepts worked, but I needed like three years to learn them rather than the allotted three days.

Bandler was brilliant, a true showman and well worth the money I paid. He could hypnotise people within seconds and even went so far as to cure a woman of her fear of snakes within minutes. At the end, I saw her petting a snake as if it were a Persian cat.

Again, as soon as I was back in the confines of my own space, the buzz created by Bandler's genius faded, and what remained was the difficulty of learning how to apply the teachings. I quickly lost interest and saw that NLP was not for me. It was very technical, and I had to learn a wide range of methods and modalities. More importantly, I felt that it was unethical for an NLP practitioner to help clients overcome phobias and fears with only ten days of certification. Surely, these people would be better served by psychologists with many years of study and training.

Not all my self-help work was worthless though. A month later, as a fully certified Bob Proctor life coach, I held a self-help seminar for forty members of my Lebanese community alongside the coach who'd first introduced me to Bob Proctor. We centred our message on the power of the mind, the law of attraction, and how to create better futures for ourselves. The seminar propelled some to continue the path of self-awareness and prompted me to give further talks. The most rewarding of these talks came when I taught a seminar to a group of teenagers—my son and his large group of friends.

I enjoyed both the teaching aspect and the elevated status speaking gave me in the community. I also found that whenever I taught or spoke about a concept, I started to internalise it much more. This would become a golden principle I'd return to often. Whenever I needed to understand a teaching, I'd either write about it or prepare a presentation to teach it. Not only would it make what I was talking about clearer, but I was also creating the right environment for the ideas to survive. In teaching what I learned, I prolonged the buzz of the seminar long enough for the lessons to become internalised.

I also started implementing daily practices that would serve me for the rest of my life. These non-negotiable rituals, as I started calling them, included rising at 5:30 a.m. every day, bar Sunday, to make room for an extra hour that I used to meditate, read, and journal my thoughts. That time in the morning was magical. Everyone was still asleep, and I'd open the window to hear the birds chirp and sing. The sun would then ascend thirty minutes later as I sat watching with a cup of coffee in my hand and a book on my lap. These four rituals—rising early, meditating, reading, and journaling—became the backbone of the transformational journey I'd undertake.

With the clarity I'd gained through my previous trials and errors, I chose my next programme and certification carefully. For a while, I'd been reading books by Brian Tracy, who was practical, business-like, and appealed to my "getting things done" manner, especially in the corporate world. I felt that I could have the greatest impact within that sphere. In September 2012, I travelled to San Diego to buy a business franchise called Focal Point that Tracy had co-developed to train corporate companies and support CEOs. Focal Point was a serious corporate training company with much success in North America. I travelled to San Diego for training and an introduction to the support team.

The training was refreshing as it was geared toward growing not only people but businesses. They had wonderful resources, templates, presentations, and a great support network. They were also teaching tangible practices that were practical and used effectively in corporate America. I also met a lot of the successful coaches there who came for an annual event. I could see how fulfilled and engaged they were in their lives. Now, I felt that I had finally latched onto something that I would love to do: to coach others in business strategy, help them grow themselves, and earn money from something different than my company. It felt that I was approaching my kind of miraculous.

As soon as I got home, I signed the franchise agreement and started a new company—Quantum Shift Coaching Solutions—aimed at serving the corporate world. At first, I did well, but then after a year or so, like with the BTBF Foundation, it tapered off. Providing such novel coaching services to narrowminded entrepreneurs in Ghana presented some unique challenges, but something else was also at play. It was me not sticking it out, not having enough grit to continue with the project. Perhaps also not having enough faith in my new self and not wanting it badly enough.

I was still making good money from my company and living a luxurious life, and I was still emotionally stuck to the old me—the businessman who was all about success, accumulation, and prestige. There was a lot of deep work I needed to do to find my peace and live a life of meaning.

At the end, the new company's challenges far outweighed the benefits, and I just couldn't give it the full attention that it needed. My main company still took a lot of time and energy out of me. Also, I found it difficult to get the right people to help me manage the new enterprise, even while monthly costs were eating away at the capital that I'd set aside for it. I found myself not having enough time to run the coaching company while keeping an eye on the foundation and managing my main company. Within less than two years of setting up the company and after serving only ten customers, I shut it down.

When it came to my unsuccessful projects, I'd always blame my failures on the circumstances. It was the fault of the new project manager at the foundation or the business customers who were not self-aware enough to want coaching. Most of all, I'd always go back and say that my main company needed me and that it was still my biggest provider in terms of money.

Therefore, it was reasonable to abandon these new heartfelt and purposeful projects I'd created.

I didn't know it then, but the failures I experienced were narrowing the path for me as I became someone new. I was changing, and so were my values. It all took much longer than I had anticipated, my unrealistically high expectations no doubt the result of gurus and social media promising instant impact.

There is an innate paradox within self-help. Its premise is that we are broken, and all the material we consume is supposed to teach us how to fix ourselves. If that is the case and we are fixed, then why do we feel that we need to jump into every seminar, listen to every podcast, and get our hands on the newest book? I didn't stop at that one illuminating lesson or book but instead became a self-help junkie.

The reality is that I was driven more by the fear of missing out and trying to sound like an expert in the field rather than wanting to use the material to actually change. I was waiting for that ultimate lesson, technique, or "satori" moment that would instantly change my life. That created an unreasonable expectation for me, so I became more anxious rather than living the fulfilled life I was seeking.

Perhaps I'd never find the answers I expected on my journey. However, the fact that I was so non-committal allowed me the freedom and intuition to delve into a trial-and-error, spiritual bucket list that addressed the big questions out there for me. My questioning was a kind of investigative reporting and, in that way, helped me delve deeper and helped others around me to ask and find answers to their own questions. I didn't feel like a poor lost soul who was hung up on new age spirituality, but rather someone in action who could help others like me.

My self-help journey showed me that there was no self-help book, seminar, or guru that could save me and that there is no end point in my personal development story. There is no miraculous purpose waiting for me on the other side. Instead, I learned that the onus was on me to do the work and use the information I'd gathered to motivate myself—but with a view of acceptance rather than saying, "Did that, so what's next?" I had gotten the knowledge intellectually. But it was now time to internalise it and understand it emotionally as well.

It was time that I took consistent and passionate actions on the ground. Time to find the practices that would help me come alive. Seen through this lens, I now realise all my failures were not really failures but rather necessary detours I had to take on my journey to understanding myself and moving toward that miraculous purpose that would help mould me into the person I wanted to become.

Chapter 4

Unlocking the Power of Vulnerability

Even with all the self-development work and the improved self-understanding that came with it, I was having a hard time putting these new, valuable principles into practice. Just as Shams al Tabriz told Rumi almost eight hundred years ago, "You must now live what you've been reading about." I knew I had to find more time for activities that made my heart purr.

Whether it was learning new principles in a Bob Proctor seminar, journaling my thoughts, reading books that stunned my mind, or speaking publicly and sharing what I'd learned, in 2012 there was an undeniable sense of aliveness that stayed with me for days on end. I wanted to chase that heightened state where everything seemed possible, so I took Annie Dillard's quote, "How we spend our days is, of course, how we spend our lives" and used it as inspiration to build a set of non-negotiables that would underpin my daily life for years to come. These practices, when I observed them consistently, filled me with contentment, magic, and a feeling of being enough. Following these habits turned principles into action, which changed my behaviour and ultimately my outcomes.

I made a New Year's Resolution to start 2013 by rising early at 5:30 a.m. every morning to prime myself for what I would do for the rest of the day—and the rest of my life. Without knowing it then, I was building small bridges that led to my heart and soul. These rituals became my spiritual oxygen, grounding me and protecting me from any negativity (especially mine) that was thrust on me.

One of these important habits was reading literary, philosophical, spiritual, and self-development books that have left their mark on the world. In the first few years, I'd read for at least an hour a day and would finish about a book a week. I found reading early in the morning meditative; it was the best time for me to comprehend words. I automatically switched off my chattering mind and focused all my energy on reading the lines on the page before me. I became lost in the details, and somehow all my worrisome thoughts fell away.

Reading opened me up to new worlds, ideas, and lives I could never have imagined otherwise. Tolstoy, Hemmingway, Hesse, Kundera, and Murakami, among others became favourite virtual mentors. I learned how life works solely from Kahlil Gibran's *The Prophet*. I know much about the slums of Mumbai even though I've never been there thanks to Gregory David Roberts's *Shantaram*.

It takes perseverance and commitment in our fast-striving lives to finish a book. In committing to read a book a week, I enjoyed having the self-control to turn away from social events or meaningless activities to instead focus on my reading. I took a book or my Kindle everywhere I went. When I felt the weekly deadline looming, I'd spend four hours on a free afternoon to make up for lost time—the striving mindset echoed in my reading too. But at least I felt fulfilled and meaningful whenever I read too much.

Though I feared I'd forget the deeper meaning of the books I'd been reading, the author's words often came to me in special moments. Or I'd recognise that I understood an idea or concept much more than I had before. It's like the good stuff would always stick. Our subconscious gets filled up with life's most precious details without us realising it.

Of course, without knowing it, all the reading led me to writing. During the Christmas holidays of 2012, I read and was inspired by Julia Cameron's *The Artist's Way*. Cameron's idea was to write three full pages in a stream of consciousness manner, which she called Morning Pages. The writing need not be coherent or have any structure, as the process of dumping your thoughts onto the page would unblock you internally and free up your creative juices.

With coffee in hand and after being sensually awakened by the nature outside my window, I'd write out my thoughts in a journal. I added my own twist to Cameron's idea by deciphering my dreams, analysing my previous day's actions, and considering in more depth the fears that were holding me back. I would also celebrate my victories, remind myself of all my good qualities, and appreciate the people and things in my life. I hardly ever went back and read my journals; once they were written, they were gone and assimilated. Over time I found that all my revelations stayed with me.

Being brought up with a lone-wolf mentality meant writing was the one form of expression I could use to self-reflect. Growing up, I never felt comfortable enough to open up in front of other people, no matter how close they were to me. I had always been shut off, afraid to express any emotion for fear of embarrassment or being hurt. I had to be alone to get in touch with the real me, and writing seemed one way to do that.

Perhaps the event that closed me off to the world was when my innocence was shattered at age eleven by a coup d'état in Ghana. It was sudden and frightening. Not least when a group of soldiers with rifles across their chests visited our house, shot a few bullets up in the sky, and demanded to see my father. A bullet hit the kitchen window on the first floor of our house in Accra. Even today, I can recall the fear I felt when I saw my father being questioned and harassed for hours.

The army, following Fidel Castro's ideology, targeted the rich, accusing them of sabotaging the country's economy and stealing its resources. That meant many businessmen were unfairly targeted. Soldiers would visit expensive homes, scaring residents for information. Luckily, my father leveraged his contacts and quickly arranged for all of us to stay at an ambassador's place. From there we soon moved to the UK to start a new life.

Suddenly, I was extracted from a comfortable, sheltered life. I was taken away from my friends, my school, and my environment and sent to a new country, England, with few people like me and few who liked me. I quickly learned that to fit into my new environment meant not to share any dark emotions like fear, shame, grief, or disappointment. I had to show that I was tough, likeable, and almost perfect—the cool new kid on the block. I could not be vulnerable, and I had to close my heart to protect myself. In doing so, I not only closed myself to the dark emotions but also to the lighter ones. I carried this way of being subconsciously well into my forties. I was all mind and reason with little room left for intuition to play any role in my life.

Little wonder then that I was now chasing activities that awakened my heart since it had been closed for so long. Both reading and writing did exactly that. In early 2012, I wrote a short story titled "Sean's Journey" about a young Irish man seeking a spiritual adventure. Both the story and the writing were poor. I didn't show it to anyone. All the same, I felt something move within me that I'd never felt before. I vowed to chase that feeling and write some more.

I started writing both short fictional stories and non-fiction self-help essays and showing them to my friends and family. I also started to post some of them on Facebook. Every time someone complimented me, I was overjoyed. Feeling alive, I kept writing, and, suddenly, at the age of forty-six, writing had somehow hijacked my life. It had become like breathing to me. It was my way of making sense of myself from the past and in the present.

I didn't write for my loved ones. I didn't write to promote my business. I wrote for me. We all need to have that *one thing* at our core—a vehicle for going deep into our essence, exploring the mysterious places of our hearts, venturing into our pasts, and confronting painful moments stored away in our subconsciouses, which had somehow in the writing process bubbled to the surface.

In Christmas of 2012, I broke my hand in a freak accident on the streets of London. I slipped on black ice while walking and fell on my fist. That meant that all my New Year's resolutions for working out in our home gym and building a better body went out the window. On my flight home to Accra, I chanced on an article about running in the plane's magazine. By the time I'd touched down in Accra at the start of the new year, I was ready to put on my running shoes.

In 2013, both running and writing would play a major role in my life. They both suited the new me that I was becoming. The one who valued experiences over material things. The one who had realised that the feeling of flow— runner's high or writer's high—superseded most feelings because it was both magical and celestial. I knew intuitively that both would help me shed the many layers blocking my invulnerable heart.

I found that running helped my writing and my writing helped my running. It was a symbiotic relationship that helped me exponentially in my self-development while quelling my inner chattering mind. Also, I think running evoked youthfulness in me, as it took me back to my teenage days when I ran cross-country at school for a short while. The freedom I'd felt then helped me get over the traumatic settling-in period I endured during the first year of my arrival in the UK. I abandoned my running as soon as most of my new friends did though. I was, after all, eager to belong to the tribe. That wouldn't be the last time I'd give up on something I liked just to appease others.

To my surprise, I realised that many writers also loved running. I was especially heartened that one of my writing heroes, Haruki Murakami, was an avid runner who regularly ran marathons. I now wanted to run a marathon.

There was a half marathon coming up in Ghana in September of 2013. As always, I read and planned how to run a half marathon thoroughly. I started my preparations in April, following a strict schedule and rising earlier than usual to avoid the torturous sun. Many times, I'd come back exhausted from the heat and humidity even at six in the morning. Luckily, June and the rainy season were fast approaching.

One morning, I got up feeling giddy. I wanted to run off some of my energy. I looked out the window, and noticed rain was imminent. Perfect conditions for running. I put on my shoes and ran toward the dark clouds filling the sky. The slight breeze suddenly picked up and became a strong wind. The trees started to shake violently, and the leaves began to scatter across the ground. I kept running. Rain pelted down from the now completely black sky. I was the only one on the road—no cars, no vendors, not even stray dogs. A chill ran down my spine and tears rolled down my cheeks. But I wasn't tired, and I didn't feel any of my usual running pains.

I was on some kind of high, and for a few minutes everything was so clear that it was as if I was at one with this universe. The swaying trees were dancing to the music from the sky, and I was the composer.

I had read *Flow: The Psychology of Optimal Experience* by Mihaly Csikszentmihalyi a few months before and now understood that what I had just experienced was "flow," the mental state of being completely present and immersed in an activity. In this state, we become so focused and absorbed in a given moment that our sense of self disappears and time and space collapse. Athletes describe it as "being in the zone." However, for me, it felt much deeper than a fleeting high. I saw it as akin to what Abraham Maslow defined as self-actualisation: "The desire for self-fulfillment, namely the tendency for the individual to become actualized in what he is potentially." I was now tapping into flow whenever I wrote or ran.

I kept true to my running plan. It wasn't easy, especially as the streets of Accra are not well equipped for running. Avoiding texting drivers, stray dogs on the streets, and long, repetitive routes was hard. I would run to an area that I'd usually driven to and expect it to cover many more kilometres than it did. What took almost thirty minutes by car and seemed like twenty kilometres turned out to be only seven and not enough for my long Sunday runs. Also, my knees were starting to hurt, and I would need regular ice baths after my long runs. This was something I'd learned from the podcasts and articles I'd started consuming on running and recovery. I'd come home covered with dirt, blood, and sweat because I had either fallen somewhere or had gotten a nosebleed. Somehow, I'd stagger into the already prepared ice bath. The first dip into the cold water was excruciatingly painful and heart stopping. After a few minutes, I got used to it, but if I moved an inch, I'd feel my heart stop again.

Come race day—the 29th of September—I was as ready as I'd ever be. I was up before sunrise and dropped off at the starting location. It was in Tema, a town thirty minutes away from Accra by car. My family would meet me at the finish line later in the morning.

The one piece of advice on running marathons that stuck with me as I read many articles and listened to other runners was that I should try and stick to my own running pace and not be overawed into running faster. Many eager runners get buzzed at the start of the race, running as hard as they can. They run at a speed and pace that not only tires them but that they won't be able to maintain for the rest of the race. The night before the race, I prepared my two-hour music playlist that would correspond with my planned pace. I also fixed my Garmin watch to guide me with my pace and speed.

When the gun went off, everyone took off as if it was a hundred-metre dash. After about thirty minutes, I was running alone, and the route took me close to the Atlantic Ocean. As I watched the sea, a few clouds moved slowly in the blue sky, and black crows circled above me—a beautiful spectacle to witness while high on adrenaline. Inexplicably, I started to cry. Not a few tears but a river was now flowing down my cheeks. I looked around to see if anyone had noticed me. Of course, no one did. Everyone was focusing on their own battle.

I didn't know it then, but it would become a regular event for me to cry when I was in a heightened state of emotion. Running always seemed to get me there. It was as if every time I ran, I'd undo the many knots that were blocking my inner self and let it out.

The race went well, and my pace matched my goal. In the last thirty minutes of the race, I started overtaking many people who shot off at the start and were now badly struggling. I immediately felt smarter when I saw their despairing faces. Then toward the end, my ego took over as I insisted on overtaking an elderly German man in his seventies who was incredibly far ahead. That wasn't clever. I stumbled and nearly fell because I was going too fast, but luckily, I recovered my composure only to watch the older man beat me.

I reached the finish line, 21.2 kilometres from the starting point, in just over two hours. I quickly stopped, dropped to the ground, and was handed a bottle of water. I just couldn't wipe the smile off my face.

When my wife and kids came to congratulate me, I ran to hug them hard. I was emotional, and the energy and excitement within me was wonderful. What I'd been chasing all along. Some of my friends also came to cheer me on, and I was so happy to see them. I had made it. I had followed the plan to the letter. The joy of that achievement stayed with me for a long time and acted as a springboard for many other events in my life. I celebrated by inviting everyone for burgers, which I'd been fantasising about since I left the starting line.

I was finally taking passionate actions that not only made me happy inside but also made me feel that I was doing things, small things, with purpose. Significantly, I was also finishing the projects I'd started. Completing the half marathon raised my self-esteem in several ways. In Walt Whitman's words, I felt larger and that I contained multitudes.

Feeling like an Olympic champion, I now wanted to run the London marathon, which was happening in April of 2014. A marathon is double the distance of a half marathon, a far more challenging and daunting task. To me it wasn't enough to run 21.0975 kilometres. I had to complete the full 42.195, which meant I had to now train for at least twelve hours a week and not the six I'd done for my first race. The training load was overwhelming as I'd be exhausted during the day and could hardly focus on work or writing. I lost the joy and started to feel anxious at night just thinking about my morning run, a stark contrast to how I'd felt when training for the first, shorter race.

Toward the end of 2013, I started having serious issues with my knees. The pain increased dramatically, and I had to abandon many training runs. I recall one morning walking back home in tears because my knee was badly swollen. I knew that my dream for 2014 was over. I went to see a doctor who told me that perhaps I'd run too much too soon. A man at my age with the history of bad knees—both have had major surgeries for cruciate ligament tears from playing football throughout my life—should have trained less than I did in the past year. Perhaps my training for the September 2013 half marathon should have been a couple of years instead of five or six months. Again, my striving mechanism made me push too fast too soon.

Though I was disappointed, I was also relieved that I could abandon the marathon attempt; it had been a heavy weight on my shoulders. Why didn't I just do things for love instead of quickly making them so competitive and turning them into goals that I had to achieve? There was something within me that needed addressing. This desire from within to feed my self-esteem by constantly achieving came from my not-enough mentality.

Though I had to abandon my hopes for the 2014 London marathon, I was still regularly tapping into the feeling of flow, becoming more emotional and regularly tearing up whenever I was running shorter distances, speaking, recalling something meaningful from my past in my journaling, or writing articles that left an impact on other people.

However, there was still something missing because everything was compartmentalised. I wasn't being myself or allowing my heart more scope in all parts of my life, especially when it came to being around people. When I watched Brené Brown's TED Talk "The Power of Vulnerability" and then read her book *The Gifts of Imperfections*, I instantly understood that my lack of vulnerability was one of the things that was holding me back. Change was not possible without involvement of the heart. Brown defines vulnerability as "uncertainty, risk, and emotional exposure. It is the core, the heart, the center of meaningful human experiences." She continues to say that "vulnerability isn't good or bad: it's not what we call a dark emotion, nor is it always a light, positive experience."

Now I knew that, until those hardened walls I'd built inside my heart broke, I wouldn't be vulnerable enough to change. My body was already ahead of my mind. Those tears on the tarmac and on my Moleskine diary was how my body was telling me that I needed to unlock the many repressed feelings I had carried within me all my life.

Inspired by Brown, I hosted a seminar titled "The Power of Vulnerability" at the Holiday Inn hotel in Accra for around fifty people, including many friends who were following my learning journey and others in the community who had started to notice my words. Many at the seminar were left baffled to learn how admitting weaknesses could be a good thing.

I explained that, like them, I'd always grown up with that mindset, but that I'd come to understand that when we do open up to the right people, we start allowing our true feelings to guide us. The more we open our hearts, the greater our capacity for empathy. The greater our capacity for empathy, the more self-aware we become. As we become more aware of the old ways that don't serve us, we let go of them and adopt new ways.

In that seminar, teaching the precepts of Brown's book to the mix of men and women, I had a moment where I truly felt that I *knew* the teaching. In that moment with all eyes on me and with a calm, fixed smile on my face, I went silent for what seemed like an eternity. It was as if life's formula was finally revealed to me. I can truly say that I lost part of my emotional shield that night.

Now running, writing, and speaking were leading me to actual change. Not just in theory. I was becoming a different person, someone who was more open, vulnerable, and full of emotions. The gates to my heart were finally opening. I was now shedding the heavy baggage that I'd been carrying since childhood.

This was exemplified a few weeks after my seminar when my son graduated from school. He would soon leave home to study at the University of Reading in England. I'd been dreading that day for so long. Perhaps my writing and running were ways to shield me from missing him.

On graduation day, I sat down in the school theatre with five hundred other parents, feeling totally alone in the dark and the quiet, with the formality of the setting slowly sinking in. It was a day of laughter and excitement for the kids and an intense mix of feelings for the rest of us. I watched him walk down the aisle with fifty other students and started to tear up without warning. I looked around—a few people were watching me—so I held myself together and watched speech after speech. I felt like I was in a daze. I did not want to break down and cry in front of all the kids and their parents. True, I was becoming more vulnerable, but I wasn't Brené Brown yet.

Next, my son won an award for achievement, and I was now convinced that this was a conspiracy to make me cry. Soon after, the ceremony ended, and the graduates threw their caps into the air. We all applauded. People were crying all around me. We took pictures and said our hellos and goodbyes and then drove off to the hotel where we were holding a shared reception with some of my son's friends.

The first thing I did was down a double vodka to calm myself—as if that ever worked. The evening was going well…until the speeches began.

I can't remember the exact words my son used, but I will never forget the feelings I felt as I watched him in front of the crowd, so grown up and confident. As I hugged him in front of all those people, my knees went weak, and suddenly the earth moved beneath me, as if time had stopped. That hug brought back memories mixed with the many emotions built up throughout the evening (perhaps enhanced by a few more double vodkas).

All in all, my heart was deeply touched with a feeling that I will never be able to explain. That hug was not just a hug. It encompassed years and years of fears, love, doubts, insecurities, heartache, hope, joy, respect, and admiration. That hug spoke a universal language understood by all, communicating directly to all the hearts in the room.

"I'm leaving you," my son was saying to me.

"I'm losing my best friend," I replied.

"But you need to let me go. I need to start my own life, my own adventure."

"I know. I understand."

I was thinking of Kahlil Gibran's words when he wrote, "Your children are not your children. They are the sons and daughters of Life's longing for itself. They come through you but not from you, and though they are with you, yet they belong not to you."

As we slowly let each other go, I noticed tears in his eyes. Then I lost all sense of my emotional control, and I cried like I've never cried before.

For me to lose control of my emotions publicly was unprecedented, but I also felt a sense of relief that I hadn't before. It was as though a veil of heaviness and sadness was being lifted. Yes, I'd miss my son terribly, but in feeling my emotions, I'd accepted his departure, and that made it okay. Not great, but okay.

Soon after the graduation party, my son left with his friends on a holiday. I was now writing much more, and with the help of a writing coach, I felt ready to start publishing a few of the pieces that I'd guarded so secretly. That ache in my heart spurred me to take the plunge and write an article. Finally, in July 2014, I wrote an article titled "The Gifts of Adversity" and sent it to *Rebelle Society*, a webzine I'd been reading. Within a week, they confirmed that they would publish it. I was astonished that they responded and even more surprised by the positive response of readers.

When *Elephant Journal* offered me a role as a featured writer, I wrote consistently for almost two years with the help of a wonderful editor, on topics that I was curious about. Titles like "What I've Learned from My Cat," "The Five Attributes of Emotional Intelligence," and "Does Your Passport Define Your Identity" made me a popular writer. I garnered almost a million views for all my articles over that two-year period. I then created my own blog and set myself a target of writing an article a week.

Toward the end of 2014, I was speaking at a telecommunications corporate event when a middle-aged woman asked, "Why would a hard-nosed businessman like yourself become a writer?"

I was taken aback and didn't know what to say to her. I finally replied with something sufficiently vague. She just nodded and sat down.

That evening after the talk, I thought about her question more seriously. I dug deeper the only way I knew how—by writing about it in a blog post.

Stephen King famously said, "Writing is refined thinking." For me, I see the writing process like making coffee. Coffee passes through many levels of refinement before arriving in our cup in liquid form. Raw beans are roasted, ground, mixed with hot water, and then finally strained and served. My thinking process starts with a particular question or thought that dominates my mind for hours and days. Especially as I run, the question percolates in my mind. I keep reflecting on it, unconsciously discussing it with myself, before finally putting pen to paper in my journal. From there, my thoughts might expand to a blog post, a social media post, or a talk. I then revise and refine again and again until I have a final product.

Writing allowed me to understand why being vulnerable and expressing myself were key to my evolution. I was also eager to share my thoughts, travails, and successes. I wanted to be heard and show my true self to the world. Writing allowed me to let down the heavy armour I'd worn since my adolescence and unveil my emotional fragility. I now recognised that vulnerability and opening my heart were not weaknesses but rather great powers that made me more connected to others and more engaged in life. I began to feel my way into life rather than sitting behind a desk and a mask as I watched life pass me by.

"And now that you don't have to be perfect, you can be good," John Steinbeck said in *East of Eden*. The thought that there is no perfection in life liberated me. I now appreciated that life is about being present and being ourselves. Now I'd have a better chance of unravelling the gems hidden beneath the many layers of my ego.

True, from the outside, I still looked divided between the softly spoken writer and the screaming "get things done" businessman. At least now there was a semblance of this new me coming out. I was in the process of solving issues and obstacles that stood in the way of my true self. Even my name changed as the new me was slowly emerging. At work and in most of my life, I'd been called by my full name, Mohammed. However, when writing, speaking, or teaching, I was called Mo. I can't remember why or how it started. But I do know that the shorter and lighter "Mo" sounded much better to me.

Dani Shapiro explains this lightness in her wonderful memoir *Devotion*:

"Yogis use a beautiful Sanskrit word, samskara, to describe the knots of energy that are locked in the hips, the heart, the jaw, the lungs. Each knot tells a story—a narrative rich with emotional detail. Release a samskara and you release that story. Release your stories, and suddenly there is more room to breathe, to feel, to experience the world."

Perhaps I found writing and self-expression late in life, but I was now breathing much better. I was now closer to authoring my life and ready to write my own stories as Mo.

Chapter 5

Unravelling My Identity

After consistently practicing the rituals that kept me connected to my inner self and the joyful activities—running, speaking, and writing—of the past year, I now recognised that I needed to release the handbrake within me and express more of myself. I lined up several such events for 2015. First, I was going to visit my son at the University of Reading to both run a half marathon with him and attend the famous Tony Robbins's "Unleash the Power Within" four-day event in London. Then there was also the small matter of my TEDx Accra talk in April, which both excited and scared me.

However, before all that, at the start of March, I travelled to Lebanon to see my aging parents and to visit the new mentor now living in my head—Kahlil Gibran. The Lebanese-American writer, poet, and philosopher explained life's most searching questions with simple, lyrical prose.

Just before boarding the flight to Lebanon, I handed my passport to the immigration officer. At the sight of my passport, he stopped laughing with his colleague and sat up.

"You are Ghanaian?" he asked mockingly.

I nodded silently. I'd heard that comment so many times that I'd grown weary of it.

"Can you speak Twi?" he asked.

"No," came my instant reply.

"Then you're not a Ghanaian," he concluded.

I was tired and not in the mood to humour him. "I was born in Ghana, lived most of my life in Ghana, and just because I look foreign doesn't mean I can't hold a Ghanaian passport," I said. "Also, for your information, I was a Ghanaian long before you were."

He was taken aback.

"You can't speak to me like this," he said. "I need to check the authenticity of your passport."

I shook my head in disbelief. I was livid. As we continued our shouting match, a crowd gathered around us. Buoyed by the support of some onlookers, the man accused me of jeopardising national security. He wanted to call the immigration police.

"Go ahead," I said.

He started furiously making phone calls.

But then a well-dressed Ghanaian man came to admonish the immigration officer. He told him it was not his job to question why I got the passport, which was the domain of the Ministry of Interior. I presumed that the man was either a lawyer or a well-known politician. The passport was real—that much was obvious—and just because I was white did not mean I couldn't have a Ghanaian passport. He continued lambasting the officer for a few minutes until the officer finally shook his head angrily and handed my passport back to me.

I took my passport, saluted the man who'd defended me, and left quickly. Despite his support, the reality was that I would never be accepted as a Ghanaian. I didn't share much of their culture or history and didn't speak their language. When other Ghanaians would discuss where they grew up, I was at a loss to share any common stories. When I heard a Ghanaian ask another which class he was at Achimota School or what hall they'd lived in, I was clueless.

On the plane, I lamented the question of my identity and shared the immigration's officer's confusion. The question of which country I belonged to had plagued me throughout my life. As a citizen of three countries—Ghana, Lebanon, and England—I had history in all of them. Yet my fellow citizens frowned upon me in all three because they didn't perceive me as an authentic national. All the thinking had made me tired, and I quickly fell into a deep sleep.

"We've arrived, sir," the hostess said as she nudged me gently.

I sat up, feeling disoriented for a few seconds. There was no one left on the plane that had just landed at Rafic Hariri Beirut International Airport. As Gibran's image floated in my mind, I quickly remembered why I was there and smiled.

At immigration, many were flagrantly colluding with the officials they knew to jump the queue while the rest of us were shaking our heads in disgust. Lebanon is the country of "wasta," which translates to knowing the right people in the right places.

When showing the immigration officer my Ghanaian passport and Lebanese ID, he got angry.

"Why didn't you fill in the landing card in Arabic?" he asked.

"Because I can't write in Arabic," I said.

"You people make my blood boil," he said. His face red, he stamped my passport silently and handed it back to me.

My parents were from Lebanon, but I'd never lived there for more than a month. Most of my friends were Lebanese who, despite living in Ghana or in other developing countries, remained part of the Lebanese diaspora. But was I truly Lebanese? On the many summer visits to Lebanon, I'd found that I had little in common with most everyone there. At lunches and dinners, while those around me reminisced about their years together at school and college, I had nothing to share, just like in Ghana. The civil war of 1975 and the political turmoil that followed affected everyone in Lebanon, but I couldn't empathise with any of them as I hadn't been there.

Gibran had also been much troubled by his country of origin, having lived outside of Lebanon for most of his life. Perhaps in visiting his village, museum, and tomb, I'd understand his plight and mine.

My question of identity was also leading me to bigger questions. I wasn't only questioning which country I belonged to but also why I was put on this earth. What was I supposed to do with my life? How would I navigate the years that I still had? These questions always reverberated in my mind. I found poets, especially Gibran, able to ease my aching. I wanted an assurance that I was at least asking the right questions. Gibran became a lighthouse that shone on the darkness within me.

In the taxi going to my parents' home, the driver complained that the political leaders were robbing the nation.

"They're all in on the game," he said, adding that politicians were cheating the people of their futures and livelihoods.

I knew that many of the four million Lebanese suffered without jobs or any kind of infrastructure and that they lived in daily fear while five or six men ruled by dividing the nation.

I loved to listen to taxi drivers because I could feel a city's vibes and secrets through them, as if they were the eyes and ears of that city. The driver's words and my own belief that the Lebanese people, through their unprincipled attitude and superficial desires, played a part in becoming victims brought some of Gibran's words to mind:

"Pity the nation that acclaims the bully as hero,
and that deems the glittering conqueror bountiful.
Pity a nation that despises a passion in its dream,
yet submits in its awakening."

I got to my parents' place quite late, but they were still up and waiting for me. Seeing them made me realise that, in doing all the internal work on myself, I wanted to dig deeper into my history too. Perhaps I'd had an unconscious tug to see them as I started to slowly release the many samskaras embedded in my being. I wanted to go back to my roots and be all alone with my parents. This time around I'd be staying with them, at their home, without my wife or kids. I'd get to spend more downtime with them, unlike in the last few years when we'd come in and leave in a hurry, seemingly busy with our kids, friends, and one social engagement or another.

My mother looked younger than her actual eighty-two years, and my father, at eighty-six, was still full of energy and life—something I envied him for. After giving me a strong hug, my mother insisted that I eat something before I slept. I settled for the lightest food that would both appease her and not affect my sensitive stomach. Labneh (a yogurt dish akin to Greek yogurt) with cucumbers, tomatoes, green olives, and Lebanese pita bread was perfect.

I awoke the next morning to the sound of my mother reciting verses of the Koran. Memories came flooding back from when I was a teenager living in England and I'd hear her strong voice early in the morning as I prepared myself to go to school. My mother was pious in a simple way, and her faith was unquestionable. She truly believed in the tenets of Islam, and her commitment to faith gave her an inner satisfaction that I have craved but never attained no matter how much I read or studied all kinds of philosophies and religions.

My father was also devout in a deeper way; he was well-versed in the intellectual aspects of Islam. He could not only recite by heart most verses from the Koran but also many of the most important Islamic scholars' work.

"Why don't you pray or fast or follow our religion properly?" my mother asked me after I told her how soothing I found her voice when reading the Koran.

"What did you expect, Mum, when we were brought up in Ghana and then the UK," I said.

She frowned, not caring for my comment.

"But what about the Arabic and Islamic teachers we hired both in Accra and London?"

"One hour a week in a strange Arabic dialect that I hardly understood was no match for my English life," I said.

The fact that neither my siblings nor I followed Islam's strict tenets was a thorn in the hearts of both my parents. Both my mother and father would always complain and implore us to read and explore the religion we were born into. However, whether it was in Ghana or England, I was surrounded by secularism—not Islam.

Perhaps unconsciously, my parents didn't like us being rooted to our history either. They tried to balance our upbringing between Western culture influence and our Islamic background. Today, when I consider the lives of other family members who were brought up in a strict religious environment, I can't help but feel fortunate. True, some feel more content with the simplicity and certainty of their beliefs, but they are also living a limited life, not scratching the surface of their possibilities. That's why I'm grateful that I was brought up in an environment with choices and an attitude of questioning beliefs and strict ideologies.

For breakfast, I had a Zaatar manoushe, a traditional staple breakfast for most Lebanese—street food that is eaten on the go, crispy on the outside, slightly chewy on the inside, and topped with a spice blend of Zaatar in olive oil. Then I went for a walk to both map the roads for my running regimen and to breathe in the Mediterranean Sea. The weather in March was beautiful (California-like) with a slight breeze that buffeted my neck and body. The wind suddenly picked up, and with it came many childhood memories about the countries I'd lived in.

Growing up in Ghana was truly romantic—my first bicycle ride, my first girlfriend, and connecting with my friends from early school years. I could still recall waking up to the sound of fufu being pounded on the wooden mortar and the aroma of groundnut soup wafting through the house and into my bedroom. Or buying kelewele (fried plantain mixed with ginger and deep fried in grimy oil) wrapped up in old newspaper sheets from the street vendors.

I'd given most of my life to Ghana, creating several businesses there. I worked mostly with Ghanaians and still have many Ghanaian friends. I knew the streets of Accra like the local I was. My children lived all their lives there, and all my family memories were in Ghana.

Then there's England. That's where I spent my formative years, from eleven until twenty-one. I could still feel the anguish of my first days at school, exacerbated by the change of weather from the certain warmth of Ghana to the uncertainty of the British climate. Rain, clouds, and cold could happen at any time, and the coldness extended to the people, too. Everyone minded their own business in contrast to the openness of the Ghanaian people. I would see the same people on the bus every day for many months, yet they wouldn't lift their faces from the newspapers they were reading even to offer a smile.

While Margaret Thatcher was fighting all kinds of men and unions in the early '80s, I was busy becoming English. I read my newspapers without looking up, ate fish and chips, and frequently ordered Indian takeaway. During my teens, football became my religion; I played, watched, and fought over it. I played snooker in the evenings and watched the BBC and ITV. Terry Wogan, Michael Parkinson, and Cilla Black became household names. I also developed my British cynicism, which I often disguised as wit or intelligence.

When I got older and went to college, London became my playground and temple of fun. I adopted it as home, but that didn't last long. At the age of twenty-one, I abruptly decided to move back to Ghana and abandon any future I had in practicing the law degree I got in England. I wanted to follow my father's and brothers' footsteps by becoming a businessman in Ghana.

On my second morning at my parents' house, I woke up early and put on my running shoes to the protests of my mother. "Who punishes himself so early?"

"I need to get runs under my belt for the half marathon race in Reading that I've planned with Nader," I said. I was still unsure if I could run, as my knees were still hurting me, but I'd leave the decision to run the half marathon or not until the last minute.

I left the apartment and quickly found the easiest route to get onto the corniche, the road that runs parallel to the Mediterranean Sea. I was surprised to see many early risers either speed walking or running. The sea beneath the rising sun was a sight to behold, and it was enhanced ten-fold when running and high on endorphins. After about six kilometres, I reached an area I'd never seen before. It was called Zeitunah Bay, a multimillion-dollar waterfront complex that included shops, restaurants, and apartments. There was also a small pier where all kinds of expensive yachts were parked. What a contrast that was to what the taxi driver was saying.

"Am I in Beirut or St. Tropez?" I thought to myself as I reflected on the ever-present divide between rich and poor—the one-dollar manoushe breakfast or the thousand-dollar Beluga caviar that filled brunches aboard the yachts.

I had a quick coffee overlooking a navy-blue yacht that must have been worth a fortune before walking back home to have breakfast with my parents. My mother had already ordered my favourite Lebanese breakfast, Kanafeh, a traditional dessert made with fine semolina dough, soaked in sweet, sugar-based syrup, and typically layered with cheese, all fitted into a baguette. Using a baguette is a modern twist to this delicacy as historically it would be served with a Lebanese street "Kaak" bread, a handbag-shaped savoury roll covered with sesame seeds—crispy on the outside and chewy a bit when eating, baked in a flame oven, and sold by cart vendors.

In the following days, I'd run or take long walks in the morning, exploring parts of Beirut I hadn't before, like an intrepid traveller visiting for the first time. This wasn't something I usually did when I came to Lebanon for summer holidays with my family. The norm would be to stay in my flat, rent a car, and dedicate my day to taking the kids out to beaches, shopping, and dropping them off at their friends' places. At night, my wife and I would live the hedonistic Lebanese nightlife with our friends. This meant frequenting the best restaurants and nightclubs and consuming a lot of alcohol. On this trip, I wanted to do more things that felt authentic to who I was now becoming. The only thing this trip had in common with my previous jaunts in Beirut was the good food that was always available.

Being on my own, talking to the real people of Lebanon, and questioning my identity meant that I was unravelling many hidden feelings inside of me, more than I'd bargained for. I reconnected with my country and its people in a way I hadn't before. I empathised with their plight and felt my stomach tighten every time a taxi driver complained about his misery. I got riled up when I heard about a top bank manager earning as little as a janitor in any average American university or when I heard that someone born into a specific religion, sect, or village would be ostracised, attacked, or could miss out on a job opportunity. It was clear that the Machiavellian political barons were getting what they wanted. When they didn't, they were ruthless in retribution.

Had the Lebanese people given up the fight, too tired or too afraid to lose the few benefits they had received from the political barons? Had they silently agreed to the terms of the devil so that they didn't have to suffer more pain? Putting myself in their shoes, I saw that they had limited options. They could follow a specific leader, which meant both believing in his selfish, power-focused cause, defending him until death, and being smitten by the gold he offered. Or they could shut their eyes, ears, and minds and follow orders—numbing their lives and living a hedonistic life without hope. That meant enjoying the moment without thinking about tomorrow. This is quite different to developing a presence where one is self-aware, intentional in one's actions, and ready to sacrifice comfort and having a good time. That was perhaps the hardest but most authentic choice.

At night, my parents and I would reminisce, with me asking them questions about the past. What was I like as a child? Why was I always alone? You were mostly happy but easily frustrated. I don't think you were lonely. You were much younger than your siblings. You were quiet and never troublesome. The answers came interspersed between meals that my mother had cooked for me. Only rarely did she allow me to order in food.

When I told my parents on such an evening that I wanted to visit Gibran's museum in Bcharre and wanted them to come with me, my father's eyes lit up. My mother tried getting out of it when she learned it was a three-hour drive.

My mother had always been aloof, not sociable, and it was always an effort for her to leave the house, to my dad's annoyance. She was rooted in her routines and rarely ventured into new terrain, whether it was going out to a restaurant or visiting family and friends. She only socialised with two or three people—her sister, brother, and his wife—unlike my father who'd talk to waiters and drivers and invite distant family members to the house.

I was my mother's son; that much was obvious. And I knew I needed to become more adventurous and open so that I could grow to be the more alive version of myself that I'd now started to nurture.

My mother relented and agreed to come with us as we set off early on a Saturday morning. After a couple of hours of easy driving, we reached the north of Lebanon close to our destination. Our car meandered through the narrow roads as we drove uphill to the Gibran's village, Bcharre. It sat on a hill 1500 metres high and overlooked Khadisha valley. Above the village, a further thousand metres, lay the highest mountain range in Lebanon, the Arez, also known as the Cedar Mountains and home to our national emblem, the cedar tree. We reached the road that led to Gibran's Museum and Tomb. As I watched the snow-covered cedar trees from afar, I got this overwhelming feeling that my trip was not only a search for my identity and spirituality but also for my future.

As I thought more, many questions came rushing to my mind. Why have all the circumstances in my life conspired to keep me away from Lebanon for so long? What is it that I disliked about it and its people that has led me to adopt other countries? Will I ever come back here to live?

Again, Gibran described the duality of my thoughts perfectly:

"You have your Lebanon, and I have mine. You have your Lebanon with her problems, and I have my Lebanon with her beauty. You have your Lebanon with all her prejudices and struggles, and I have my Lebanon with all her dreams and securities. Your Lebanon is a political knot, a national dilemma, a place of conflict and deception. My Lebanon is a place of beauty and dreams of enchanting valleys and splendid mountains. Your Lebanon is inhabited by functionaries, officers, politicians, committees, and factions. My Lebanon is for peasants, shepherds, young boys and girls, parents, and poets. Your Lebanon is empty and fleeting whereas My Lebanon will endure forever."

I didn't have to live in the land of Lebanon to be Lebanese. Why couldn't I belong to the land even if I wasn't living there? There were more Lebanese people (six million) living outside the country than living in Lebanon (four million). Many had been forced to seek greener pastures in other countries because Lebanon had been hijacked by warlords who used religion to weaponise the divide and garner their votes. I was Lebanese, spoke Lebanese-Arabic, ate the "Zaatar" manoushe most mornings, and enjoyed listening to *Fairuz* whenever I was feeling melancholic. I also have many Lebanese traits, like generosity, an open and hospitable house, my entrepreneurial spirit, and of course my big nose. Also, like many Lebanese, I regularly complain about Lebanon.

The museum was in an old monastery high up in the village. At the entrance stood a huge granite statue of Gibran. Getting to the entrance meant a steep walk up many steps. My mother's lack of mobility meant it would be too hard for her to make the effort. She decided to stay in a nearby cafe that was at ground level. My father didn't want to leave her alone, so he stayed with her.

As I entered the museum alone, I started to understand the real Gibran and imagined how he had led his life. He wasn't just a writer of beautiful words or a painter of breathtaking pictures but a messenger from some higher place who came to serve as a reminder, as an exemplar, and as a guide to us mere mortals. His message was simple: that we were beautiful souls having a human experience and that we were united in this experience called life. He communicated in a language that addressed our hearts, directly removing the need for our analytical minds.

I reached his tomb and read his epitaph: "I am alive like you, and I now stand beside you. Close your eyes and look around you. You will see me in front of you."

I was overcome, and tears rolled down my cheeks like a summer thunderstorm that erupts without warning. I was truly moved, and I felt something stir deep within me. I felt I had someone looking out for me. I felt like I wasn't alone. I felt like my heart had expanded. I felt like I was all-knowing. I felt absolute peace. And most of all, I felt totally loved. Finally, I felt I belonged to Lebanon.

As I left the museum and stood outside, gazing at the valley beneath me and the snow-covered Cedar Mountains above me, I continued to have this peaceful feeling from within. I was intoxicated with that "wine of life" Gibran kept referring to.

I walked down to a spot by some cedar trees and just sat in awe of them for a few minutes. I could swear they were talking to me, inviting me to come closer and observe how simply they lived. I wondered if they were trying to tell me that they knew where they belonged, in this mountain range, in this Lebanon. Later in the evening, I'd write in my journal:

> *We go through tough times in winter when it is cold, and we face strong and abrasive winds. We shed our leaves and our seeds and stand naked, yet we stand tall. We also go through the spring where we grow our seeds and leaves, and we stand beautiful and tall. However, throughout the year, we stand together, grateful, joyful, and accepting of what comes our way.*

I caught up with my parents, and we went to a well-known restaurant that specialised in a local delicacy called "Kibbeh"—a mixture of bulgur wheat, onions, and ground beef that forms a hollow shell for a delicious stuffing.

Enveloped in warm and earthy Middle Eastern spices like allspice and ground cinnamon, kibbeh is the epitome of Middle Eastern comfort food.

I explained to my parents what Gibran had meant to me and that I wished they could have seen his works. I showed them the many pictures I took and chronicled his life story to them. They now looked tired and wanted to head back home. It was rather ironic that neither of them entered Gibran's mausoleum—as if my spiritual path was separate and completely different to theirs. While they followed and were at peace with Islam, I was growing to be at peace with the language of Gibran, the poets, and their ilk.

The drive back was long, lonely, and sad. The good energy had left me, replaced by a creeping self-doubt and despair. Soon these thoughts were like an invisible force with a will of their own, whispering and spreading rumours inside my mind, wiping away all the peace I had found earlier that day.

I had reached a crossroads in my life. I had to make some tough decisions. Who would I become in the next stage of my life? I felt like I was living a double life, caught between the spiritual and material worlds. Could I run my business and still be a writer/speaker of the "good life?" I found it difficult to fuse both realms into one life, and that made me feel lost, confused, and frustrated. That feeling tapped directly into my greatest fear—that I would live a mediocre life, far away from my country, my tribe, and my true essence, only realising on my deathbed that I chose the easy way instead of the more authentic one for me.

Gibran was born with a talent, yet he endured much pain; he had to leave his native country early in life. His mother, sister, and brother all died within a year of each other. However, he found the strength to live alone in New York and sacrificed himself for the love of his work. He would often write or paint for hours, without eating or taking a break. He lacked both the time and resources to visit his beloved Lebanon and instead spent all his time producing the masterpieces that he did. However, he found his unique way and carved his own niche in the psyche of Lebanon.

The night before I travelled home, I read Gibran again and stumbled upon these words:

"Say not, 'I have found the truth,' but rather, 'I have found a truth.' Say not,' I have found the path of the soul.' Say rather, 'I have met the soul walking upon my path.' For the soul walks upon all paths. The soul walks not upon a line; neither does it grow like a reed. The soul unfolds itself like a lotus of countless petals."

Gibran was telling me that I should never forget my spiritual essence, no matter which part of the Earth I was born into or resided in. That was my true identity. His words and my thoughts met for a timeless second and painted one single thought: life was all about the discovery of our inner self. It was about asking questions, and ultimately, it was about asking the right question that was particular to me. Only then could I start living the answers.

On my last day in Lebanon, my mother cooked for me one final time. As the day passed by and light became dark, I felt sad. I'd seen and felt how my parents had aged and rued the fact that I hadn't being seeing enough of them. I vowed to myself that I'd visit more often, not knowing then that I'd be back in only three months' time.

On the plane back, once again my thoughts drifted toward identity. Should our passports define our identities? In the last thirty years or so, many borders have fallen or been redrawn. As a new word—globalisation—has emerged, a new world has blossomed with it. The cultural concept of identity that we have is faulty, extremely limiting, and prone to drive us into conflict.

Identity is not as simple as your passport but rather very complex. It is not static; it is fluid, always changing according to context and individual dynamics.

The thought that we are each continually creating our own identity assured me in my path. I was not striving when it came to my self-expression, but rather reinventing myself. As I've immersed myself in the writing world in the last several years, I've found myself relating more with people who have a literary interest than those who speak my language. It doesn't matter to me whether they are from China, Kenya, or Belgium. I am much more likely to open my heart to someone who reads Bukowski, Gibran, or Murakami than a person whose country I happen to share.

Today, I feel more a citizen of the world—bound to others by my values, interests, passions, and beliefs rather than the colour of my skin, flag on my passport, or the street where I grew up. This is who I am today, but that doesn't mean it's who I will be tomorrow. We human beings have become much more intricate, a mosaic of world systems and beliefs. We are constantly reinventing ourselves. We're all becoming citizens of the world, so it's time to understand what that means.

Watching the sun appear on the horizon of my plane window, I smiled as Gibran's words came to me. We were all descendants of peasants and shepherds. We were all once young boys and girls who, deep in their hearts, were all poets, living in a land of beauty full of dreams and insecurities that will endure forever.

I am a peasant.

I am a poet.

I am a shepherd.

Chapter 6

Unleashing the Power Within

It was finally time to visit my son. I arrived in London toward the end of March and took a train to Reading and a taxi to the university campus. Nader, my son, was waiting for me so that we could run the Reading half marathon the next morning. My running had been sporadic since the doctor confirmed my worst fears about my knees. There was no way I could run the race. But I hadn't told Nader.

"I won't be running the race," I blurted out after getting out of the taxi.

"What? Are you kidding me," he said.

"My knees are killing me whenever I run long distances. I won't be able to run ten kilometres let alone twenty-one," I said.

He frowned, his face sullen with disappointment. "Dad, you must try. We were supposed to do this together."

I nodded, remembering why I had dreaded having this conversation. "Okay, let's see how I feel tomorrow morning."

As we walked through the open and green campus, I asked him whether he had prepared as I'd advised.

"Don't worry. I'm ready," he said. We spent the rest of the day together as he showed me around his university and introduced me to some of his friends. The next morning, I arrived to pick him up and go by taxi to Madejski Stadium, the race's starting and ending point.

"I don't get you. Why am I even running," he said, visibly upset, when he saw me without my running gear.

"Honestly, I can't run. I wish I could. I promise you in a few years we will get to run together," I said. "I'm also sad that I don't get to run with you, but I don't want to be humiliated out there on the roads when my knees give way." I felt terrible but wanted him to run, to experience that feeling of flow that can be amplified on race day.

"Fine, I'll run," he said.

I was disappointed with myself for letting him down. I guess that was an instance when he had to witness his not so perfect dad pulling out of a fight.

Over time, I'd been sharing running advice with him, but on the way to the stadium, I found out he hadn't followed any of it. The running shoes he was wearing looked worn out and uncomfortable. I shook my head in disbelief. To add insult to injury, he told me he'd also stayed up late the night before.

At the starting point, I stopped giving him advice and let him be. Two hours later he would arrive at the Madejski Stadium, strolling through his final lap as if he'd gone for a Sunday walk. All my thinking, analysis, and worries were for a middle-aged man, not for an athletic eighteen-year-old. I hugged him hard and saluted his casual manner, which I have always admired in him. He's the opposite of me. Even at such a young age, he had more composure than I did.

A few days later, he forgave me as our focus shifted to the Tony Robbins "Unleash the Power Within" event. We were both looking forward to walking on fire and "overcoming the unconscious fears that were holding us back," as Robbins's site proclaimed. We arrived early at the ExCel Center in Royal Victoria Dock, a huge complex that hosted many of the world's leading events, and were quickly shown to our "gold package" seats very close to the stage. The energy in the arena was incredible, with more than ten thousand participants in the audience from every part of the world clapping, dancing, and screaming.

Right on time, Robbins came charging on stage to the sound of loud pop music. He was two metres tall, weighed at least 120 kilograms, and was built like a tank. He looked like Arnold Schwarzenegger, but even bigger. Over the next twelve hours, Robbins exuded incredible passion and stamina, asking us to question our belief systems in so many ways.

"Today is when you decide to change. Today is when you start operating from a new belief that says life happens not to me but for me," Robbins screamed into the mic.

He spent the rest of the day explaining that we are a result of our belief systems, which are made up of our worldviews and the set of rules we live by. All of these were handed down to us by our parents or primary caregivers. These beliefs were driven by two main fears: "We are not enough" and "We won't be loved."

After my Lebanon trip where I'd questioned my identity and which country was truly my own, I was now ready to question the belief system that had been running my life since childhood. True, I'd made progress since 2010 and the Bob Proctor event, but this time around I was going deeper.

On that first day, Robbins kept going for eight hours non-stop, and at 6:00 p.m. we got a short break. After that, with music blaring in the background, he spent the next six hours priming us and readying our minds for the fire walk. He kept repeating what great minds we had and how much potential we had within us. In a maniacal frenzy, minutes before we embarked on the walk, he energised us into a peak state so that we felt invincible. He then asked us to remove our shoes and leave them near our seats.

I turned to my son. "Barefoot. It's bloody cold."

"Look at everyone around us." He smiled, pointing to the crowds taking off their shoes.

Though my son had inherited my reserved nature, he was hyped up and in a cheerful mood. We followed the group out of the arena to the car park outside, screaming, "Yes! Yes! Yes!"

In front of us, the space was divided into several sections that encompassed five-metre lines of the red-hot coal. Helpers were everywhere, at the start, finish, and on the sidelines. My feet were now freezing from the twenty minutes' walk we needed to reach the simmering coals.

I thought of the advertising slogan that sold me on the event: "Once you start doing what you thought was impossible, you'll conquer the other fires of your life with ease."

Was that true? What was the point of all this? What if I burned my feet? Or, worse, my son burned his.

"The red-hot coal can reach up to two thousand degrees," a man who'd been sitting behind us said.

But that thought was drowned out by the buzz around me as team Robbins urged us to keep moving. Throughout the day, whenever Robbins pumped us with positive talk like, "You're invincible" or "You're full of possibilities," he would recite the phrase, "Cool Moss. Cool Moss. Cool Moss." He was using a hypnosis technique where he'd anchor our positive feelings with that phrase, placing a kind of bookmark in our subconscious that hyped us up when we needed it most, at the fire walk.

After we walked on damp grass for a short distance, I found myself at the head of one of the pits. I'd be the first one from our group to walk on the burning coals. I had little time to question if anchoring worked or if I was invincible. I followed the instructions, acted out my rehearsed power move, and recited "cool moss, cool moss, cool moss." I glanced behind me at my son, gave him a reassuring look, took a deep breath, and walked forward toward the five-metre path of hot, smouldering coals laid out in front of me.

Blistering heat emanated from the amber coals. I marched on, walking onto the fire with my bare feet.

It was brief. I felt no pain.

All I could see were the excited faces of Tony Robbins's team urging me on. As soon as I arrived at the end of the strip, the crew members quickly hosed off my feet and between my toes to make sure that there weren't any loose coal pieces stuck there.

I didn't have time to reflect on what I felt because it was my son's turn.

But I couldn't watch. It was one thing if I burned my feet while following my passion, but I wouldn't forgive myself if something happened to my son.

Instead, I turned around and only faced him when he reached the end. He had this big smile on his face and was oblivious to any of the worries I'd felt. To him, it was easy, like the half marathon had been.

We high-fived and screamed, "We did it."

Today, I still can't comprehend how we walked on fire. Often, when I light a cigar with a match, I can sense the heat from the flame. Fire, heat, flames–they burn you. Was the coal laid out fake? Was Tony Robbins a magician like the famous David Copperfield? Everything looked and seemed legitimate. Oprah Winfrey had done the walk and aired it to millions. Who was I to question Robbins when Oprah Winfrey gave him a thumbs up?

Later, when I read up on the fire walk, I found that walking on damp grass just before we stepped onto the fire gave us a protective layer for seconds. Plus, the speed we walked when egged on by the assistants meant we didn't keep our feet in one place long enough to get burned. Perhaps that was an explanation.

However, the whole point of the walk was metaphorical. Once we conquered our fears, nothing was impossible. We were capable of much more than we believed. Though I didn't realise it then, the walk broke some internal barrier in me that gave me the confidence to tackle any future challenge, specifically my upcoming TEDx Talk, without fear. Perhaps, if the Reading half marathon had come after the Tony Robbins event, I might have attempted it.

The third day with Robbins was called "Transformation Day." We had already conquered our fears on day one with the fire walk. Then we clarified our life's vision and created a plan for it on day two. Now the only thing standing between us and our dreams were our limiting beliefs. When we did some clarifying exercises, I could clearly see the raging internal battle between my inner child screaming that I wasn't good enough and the new "Mo" who was calmly reassuring me that I was.

True, I had come a long way from 2008, growing in self-awareness after kicking the anti-depressants, finding the practices that gave me inner joy, and finally expressing my muted voice. But I still struggled with some limiting beliefs that stood tall as obstacles to who I wanted to become. It was too easy for me to default to comfort, and thus I sometimes lacked the hunger and passion to finish plans. I was still too affected by what people thought of me and wasn't letting go of my materialistic lifestyle. Finally, I still needed to be extraordinary instead of embracing the ordinary, simple, and mindful aspects of life.

The biggest insight I got with the high music blaring and Robbins's voice screaming at me was that these four limiting beliefs I'd endured since becoming an adult would remain with me until I stopped letting them control me. But this would be my life's work, not something I could do after one or two events. Most importantly, the way to reduce them and change exponentially was to get out of my comfort zone and get into action.

There was a lot of hype surrounding the UPW event, with high-fiving and fist-pumping almost compulsory. It almost left me wondering if I had just arrived at a rave in Ibiza. Ultimately though, I left with an incredible feeling and a knowing that anything was possible. It was a once-in-a-lifetime spectacle. Of all the self-help teachers and seminars I've visited, I'd say that Tony Robbins's was the best. He truly is a force of nature. Not because of his content, since at the end of the day most self-help is the same, but because of his personality and raw energy. It was as if, with his non-stop dynamism, he beat us into submission so that we faced and conquered our fears.

A few days after the UPW event, I travelled back to Ghana and still had the little matter of a TEDx Talk that I had agreed to give six months earlier. My enthusiasm for speaking on the TED platform started almost a year prior when I saw the inaugural TEDx Accra. I arranged to meet the young organisers and understood what it would take to speak. I wanted desperately to speak in front of a large audience, especially at such a prestigious and well-known event. I was in full striving mode, using all my connections to get an invite. As I questioned my limiting beliefs during the UPW event, I felt embarrassed at the way I went about getting the TEDx invite. However, I also felt it would be a cop out if I did cancel for that reason.

A week before the event, after rehearsing and impressing the TEDx committee and a speaking coach, it was decided that I'd be a main speaker. The decision justified the way I'd used all means to get on the list of speakers, but now the pressure was on. I was filled with such trepidation that I wanted to withdraw many times during the week before the official date. However, the Robbins event had taught me that I could achieve more than I knew. Giving up was not an option. I decided that I was going to step up in all areas of my life. I told myself that this talk was the start of the real change I wanted to embark on, not the intellectual change I'd been unwittingly stuck in.

Though I regularly spoke in front of people, this was different. Not only was it TEDx, but it was also very personal, as I would bare my soul in front of everyone. The title of the talk was "Rich, Successful, and Strong—Yet Empty." I would be admitting to family, friends, and strangers that for most of my adult life I'd been following the wrong values. I would be explaining my new self-awareness and what was behind the new tears and laughter that were now apparent within me. I was also, in a way, telling the friends and family I'd grown up with that I didn't believe in their values anymore. The stakes had never been higher for me.

As the day grew nearer, my sleep got more erratic. I would remind myself every morning that I had decided on it, I was committed to it, and I was going to give it my best. I practiced my talk as if my life depended on it. I repeated it five or six times. I made my family listen to me practice, and then I went to work and forced my employees to hear me out as well. The more I practiced, the less fear I held.

On the big day, many things went disastrously wrong. My talk was delayed for two hours because the technical team were disorganised. The stage lighting and the cameras had not been set up correctly. But I didn't let any of that get to me.

Twenty minutes before the talk, I used what I'd learned at the UPW event to put myself in a positive state, reminding myself of the Robbins quote: "Where our focus goes, our energy flows." I breathed in through my nose and out through my clenched mouth for ten minutes. I then listened to some music and recited an affirmation that I'd prepared specifically for the talk, which started with "Say Yes. Say Yes to defying the odds" and ended with "Step up. Step. Step up." Yes, it was cheesy, but it worked.

As soon as I got on stage, I panicked. Everything went into a blur for a few seconds until I remembered to breathe again for a few more seconds. Then, as I started to get into my rhythm, the screen showing my presentation slides went blank. Then the timer screen to my right, which acted like a guide so I could pace my talk, also went blank. I faltered for a few seconds but then took another deep breath and told myself I was going to do this and that the worst had passed. All my preparations kicked in, and I spoke without needing the slides or the timer:

"In Tolstoy's book *The Death of Ivan Illich*, Ivan lays down dying after leading a colourless, mediocre life, and he has one thought: What if I had lived my entire life wrong?

"I read this book in the midst of my depression, and it was a catalyst to my transformation. I used to be someone who was angry and would fret at the simplest of things. I used to do everything very quickly and not even pause to understand why I was doing it. That all changed.

"I was brought up in a way that is not too dissimilar from most people. I was loved and taught how to behave within our society, how to differentiate between what was right and what was wrong. These rules of behaviour or beliefs were inadvertently passed onto me. Usually by my parents, teachers, community, and the environment around me. Over time, these beliefs crystallise into stories and, if left unchecked, become life-defining stories which run our lives.

"One such story that defined me was the formula of success and happiness. The belief of my father and his forefathers was very simple; you worked hard, settled down, got married and raised a family, made money, enjoyed spending some of the money, followed the rules of society, and gained social prestige…"

Toward the middle, I teared up as I explained the pain of feeling empty even though I'd done everything I thought I was supposed to do.

My time on stage passed so quickly. I missed the light that meant I should stop, and only realised it when I saw the face of one of the organisers. I knew I had to wrap it up.

"Aliveness is something that is unique and different to each one of us, and it need not be a revolution that changes your life completely. But it very often is a slight tweak where you add certain things that make you come alive.

"I'm not against making money. I see it as a means to an end and something that we need to fulfil our basic need for security. However, I do believe that we need self-growth and contribution to our fellow man before our lives can become meaningful.

"What I'm trying to say is that we can't wait like Ivan Illich 'til our deathbeds to question whether we lived our lives wrong. I'm saying go find that thing that you want to wake up to every morning. There is a book that is waiting to be written, there is a song waiting to be sung, and there is a new business start-up waiting to happen. Go awaken your aliveness so you can participate fully in this wonderful game called life."

I ended my talk to rapturous applause.

As I left the stage and went to a common area outside, I was approached by Patrick Awuah, the founder of Ashesi University in Ghana and one of *Fortune*'s top fifty leaders in the world for 2015. He thanked me for my talk and told me how inspired he was by my words. He had heard about me and my Born to Be Free Foundation and wanted to know if we could work together in some capacity. I would reach out in a few years to start another initiative.

I felt so emotional, was on the biggest high I'd ever experienced, and I really understood what Tony Robbins must have felt like during his fourteen hours of marathon talks. I wanted to cry there and then, and when I saw my daughter coming toward me, I gave her one of those million-dollar hugs as tears rolled down my cheeks.

In the following few days, I was filled with a sense of relief I had never experienced before. The weeks that followed saw my belief, confidence, and energy rise to a level I never knew I had. It was as if I had overcome some big and inhibiting fear by simply getting into action and doing the talk. I had climbed Mount Everest and come back alive.

I was now invited to speak at business events and some teaching institutions, where I spoke about spirituality, self-development, and my transformation. I also got active on social media, which launched me into the Ghanaian limelight. Now people were appreciating me and noticing me much more than I was used to. I started to bask in the glory of it all.

My "not enough" mentality from childhood meant that I was allowing my new mini-celebrity status to get to my head. That ignored child within me was enjoying having his own voice. But at the same time, doing so many things and getting comfortable with being uncomfortable meant that I was growing. By taking action, I was releasing many internal stories inside of me and venturing toward the real authentic me—I was unleashing the power within.

Chapter 7

Learning to Surrender

Still riding high from my TEDx success, I was not prepared for my phone to ring on July 11th with bad news.

"Andrus has passed away," Bassam said.

My extroverted brother Bassam was always abreast of all the news around us. We hadn't been close growing up. He was older and focused on himself. Even so, our shared lifestyles, values, and the fact that our wives were close meant that we spent most of our time together as adults and became closer.

"What? How could he just die so suddenly," I said, stopping the car and parking aside.

It wasn't like Andrus was my best friend or someone I'd see regularly, but he was part of my tribe—a third-generation expatriate Lebanese living in Ghana. His family was one of the original Lebanese families who had emigrated to Ghana in the early twentieth century—not the ones who flooded in afterwards. He had grown up in Ghana and our parents knew each other since the '50s. We got married to our respective wives in the same month. We had many mutual friends, and our kids went to the same school and became friends. We would always meet at big social occasions and especially at Ada, the riverside location we both frequented on the weekends.

Andrus had collapsed while on a cruise ship with his family off the coast of Nice and was taken quickly to a hospital nearby. At first, doctors said it wasn't serious, but then he became progressively worse in the hospital. A few nights later, he suddenly passed away. The hospital couldn't find any answers, but finally, they said it was heart failure.

I was saddened and shocked by his death. That day remains etched into my memory like one of those "where were you when JFK was shot" moments.

For days on end, his innocent smile wouldn't leave my mind. I kept thinking of his wife and children. How would they handle his death at such a young age, just forty-eight years old? How much life would he miss? He was a few months older than I was. Perhaps that's why his death had affected me so much. It was the first time that someone I knew had actually died.

Though Reda's near-death experience marked me emotionally, Andrus's death hit me existentially. The suddenness of it all made me feel so fragile, as if life could turn on me in a second. The next day, I wrote in my journal:

> *It's time to cut the bullshit and start planning my life as if death is perched on my shoulder. Enough of the self-analysis, recriminations, and fear of taking action. Enough questioning my every past move. It's time I wake up, get serious, and create a concrete plan that covers the future. One that can take care of my children in case something happens to me. It's time to put dates on the calendar of all the big moves I'm dreaming of—leaving Ghana to live on a Mediterranean island, becoming an accomplished writer, and, most importantly, living a much simpler life.*

Before I could truly embark on implementing some changes to live more simply, however, I got another phone call from Bassam, this one just five days after the first.

"Mum's been rushed to hospital with what could be a blood clot," he said.

"What?" I mumbled quietly. I was at a dinner party and flashed my wife a serious look as I stood up to leave.

"It's serious. You should fly down immediately," he said.

"Okay," I said.

We quietly made our excuses to the hosts and went home. On the way, I called the travel agency to get me on any immediate flight to Lebanon. I was a bit anxious but not too worried as my mother was healthy and I'd just seen her a few months back.

A few hours later, just as I was walking to bed, Bassam's number flashed up on my phone. My heart immediately sank.

"Our mother is gone," he said.

I couldn't say a word. I fell to my knees, and immediately tears flooded my cheeks as I wept like a child. My wife walked in on the news and quickly ran to embrace me as I cried uncontrollably on her shoulder. Then my son, who was visiting us in Ghana, also came to embrace me too. I felt as if the ground had shifted under me. I couldn't believe the speed of how it all happened.

I called Imman, my sister, who was in hysterics.

"At least she didn't suffer and went quickly," I said, trying to soothe her.

My comment felt so stupid. I just didn't know what to say anymore. Still today, I regret those words coming out of my mouth.

"There was nothing wrong with her. It's not fair how she quickly she died," Imman said.

The next morning, it seemed that everyone knew. I was receiving calls of condolences, something I wasn't comfortable with. By late morning, together with my older and more stoic brother Hassan, we found seats on the plane flying off to Beirut.

My older brother was quiet and rarely expressed emotion. I can't even recall us hugging when we met up at the airport. We were both in pain. We both knew the drill, so what was the point of sharing that in front of others? It was a silent conversation between us.

The only two seats we could find on the flight were jump seats the air crew used for taking off and landing. I'm not sure if other airlines allowed for normal passengers to use them, but I knew it was a normal occurrence on Middle East Airlines (MEA), Lebanon's only airline company, especially during summer when flights were always overbooked with many Lebanese flocking back home.

The flight was hard, especially since there was no privacy and everyone who knew us kept coming up to extend their condolences. As soon as we arrived at Beirut, we took a car to my father's house in the south.

My mother would be buried in Tyre where both she and my father were from. Islamic custom meant that the body had to be buried within twenty-four hours of death.

When I saw my father, my shield dropped, and we both cried as we embraced. He was a broken man, and his frail figure tore my heart apart. It didn't get any easier when I met Imman, who was not taking it well. She had been in Lebanon, visiting from Kuwait where she worked, when my mother was taken to hospital.

I was anxious about the upcoming funeral and all the unfamiliar traditions that came with an Islamic burial. I also wasn't looking forward to the many people who would be coming to pay their respects.

That night, I slept upstairs in one of the many rooms of my father's house while, unbeknownst to me, the body of my dead mother was lying downstairs. As morning came, the proceedings began. I went down to where my mother lay covered in only a white cloth on a special platform. Close relatives recited passages of the Koran to her, and others wailed loudly. The room was filled with mainly women, including aunts, nieces, and other distant cousins.

Custom meant that we had to carry the body to a waiting hearse, which would then drive her to the cemetery with several cars in a convoy behind all driving at low speed. I was taken aback by the tumult that now surrounded us. Not knowing what to do next, I was ushered over to my mother's body so that I could help carry her. I approached her body and felt uneasy trying to lift her. I saw the rest doing so without question and followed suit. As I lifted her, I felt her head brush against my leg. I was petrified. The sensation of her touch and the squeamish cries, shrieks, and screams in that large room where my mother lay made me feel uneasy.

Islamic tradition dictated that the men would carry the body to the burial site while the women stayed at home. Imman got upset as she fully expected to go to the burial. She had to be calmed by one of our aunts, who reiterated the rules for her.

I carried on walking with the rest of the men as we carried my mother's body to the waiting hearse. After we put her in the hearse, I got into one of the cars behind it and drove slowly for about ten minutes until we arrived in the town centre. The two roads leading to the cemetery were closed now, honouring one of their own, my beloved mother.

I got out of the car into the scorching heat, still wearing a dark suit, and found myself surrounded by hundreds of men. The heat and mayhem made me feel like I was suffocating, and I had to take several deep breaths. A distant relative or perhaps a stranger told me, in no uncertain terms, that I was supposed to hold the body. I did so for a few minutes until I was pushed aside by stronger men. We walked for about another ten minutes down the meandering road that led to the cemetery, which was close to the old Roman ruins on the outskirts of the city centre.

Finally, we arrived at the burial site, and peculiar faces I'd never seen before surrounded me. My brothers, Hassan and Bassam, were close by while my father stood hidden behind those strange men. We walked down some awkward steps until we arrived at where my mother would be lain.

I had been to some funerals before but had always switched off. I would think of anyone but the person who died or their grieving family. That way, I avoided the pain. This time around, though, I just couldn't wipe away the image of my mother's face or the pain I felt. I just wanted it to end.

I can recall today that her body was lowered into the hole—laid bare, not in a coffin. There was much reading of the Koran, which was the most soothing aspect of the whole experience. Then, there was a reception near the burial site where I shook the hands of what seemed like a thousand men of whom I knew only a handful.

We returned to my father's house around lunchtime and were met by my wife, who had arrived on another flight. Her presence comforted me as a companion and as someone who could help translate these customs I was enduring. My wife had lived a large part of her life in Lebanon, had witnessed these rituals many times, and adhered closer to the tenets of Islam than I did even though she wasn't the fully practicing Muslim my mother expected.

The next few days and weeks were spent receiving people paying their respects. I found myself transported to another planet. I was physically there but not mentally. By now, my eleven-year-old invulnerable mentality had kicked in, and I was in total control of my feelings. This was my game, one that I had learned so expertly when I moved to England. Over the next few days, weeks, and months I showed little emotion and suppressed most memories of my mother. I wanted to be strong for everyone, especially my father. I pushed the pain to a place in my heart that was barely visible. A new samskara had now formed in my body, something I knew was not good for the new version of Mo, but still, I couldn't stop acting that way.

Slowly things returned to usual as they always do. Our lives moved on quickly without my mother. I couldn't help but feel that though we were all in pain, my father more than any of us, at least we were still alive. My mother was gone—with us no more. That was the saddest aspect. She was not forgotten completely, but she was slowly fading from our memories.

My dad decided to leave the hustle and bustle of Beirut, the home he had shared with my mother. He wanted to be closer to his side of the family in Tyre, and he also wanted to live in the big, lovely house that he had built years ago. My mother had always resisted living in that house and in the south full time and would only go there on weekends. She was pious and felt that my father's family were too radical and cultish in their faith and didn't want them to be fully part of her life. However, with all his children returning to different countries, my father had no one around him. Moving to the south was a sound choice.

My family and I cancelled our planned summer trip to the United States and instead stayed in Beirut for the summer. Our plan had been to meet up with my daughter, Savannah, who was in an art summer camp at NYU in New York. She had missed the funeral, but now she would come and stay with us in Beirut. We wanted to spend the whole of August in Lebanon in order to be near my father and help him move to his new home.

On a whim, I sold my riverside retreat in Ada, Ghana and used the money to buy land in Lebanon. Looking back now, both Gibran's take on Lebanon and my mother's death helped me plan, without knowing it, for a celestial home, a place where I'd one day retire. The land I bought echoed much of Gibran's Lebanon as it overlooked several valleys, hills, and rivers. Standing over the land, I could see myself as a sixty-five-year-old, with coffee in hand, writing my thoughts in a journal. I'd also subconsciously wanted us to quit our role as the social hub for everyone back home. I was tired of hosting people at my riverside retreat, especially now that neither of my kids had much use for it.

Soon after my mother's death, my sister prompted me to see a faith healer she knew. We both shared an interest in spiritual healers and everything occult. She was also worried I was holding onto my grief instead of expressing my pain and thought that maybe this faith healer could help.

I arrived at the faith healer's apartment a few minutes before my appointment. She opened the door and smiled—not in a creepy way, but pleasantly. She looked more like a corporate executive than a faith healer, but her name was Shisha. She had strength in her eyes and a compelling aura about her.

We exchanged pleasantries, and I entered the healing room. It was functional, the walls a fresh white interspersed with dashes of colour. A bookcase displayed works by Rumi and Kahlil Gibran as well as books I had read on my self-discovery journey like *Conversations with God* by Neal Donald Walsh. A thick white moquette covered the floor. Predictably, there was incense burning, and some neoclassical music played in the background. The scent and sounds eased me into a peaceful but surreal place.

We sat facing each other, and she softly asked me why I had come. I said that my mother had passed away twenty days before and that I didn't know how to feel. She smiled and looked at me for a long time. She dimmed the lights and asked me to get up onto the massage table. I lay on my back, and she whispered to me to close my eyes while she asked the divine for Reiki energy to flow through her. Within a few minutes, I fell into an in-between place; I wasn't asleep, but I wasn't awake either.

I could sense her bare hands hovering above my body. Energy flowed through her hands into my neck, throat, shoulders, stomach, and legs. A hot, tingling sensation moved throughout my body.

After about twenty minutes, I started coughing violently. She asked me to sit up and gave me a glass of water to clear my throat. I then lay on my stomach for her to continue and fell into a deep sleep.

Her soft nudge woke me.

"Hope you're feeling better," she said. I slowly got up and came to sit in front of her. I drank a few sips of the hot green tea she offered. She asked me to describe what I'd felt, and I told her about the in-between place and the tingling sensations.

"When you coughed, there was something stuck in your throat chakra. It was a message that needed to come out to you," she said.

"Oh really," I said.

"It was your mother, talking from the other side."

"Oh really," I said again, starting to feel awkward.

We were now getting into woo-woo territory. Yes, I was into self-help and spiritual ideas, but I was startled when it was directed at me.

"Your mother wanted to tell you to look up the story of Zachary in the Koran."

"I'm not religious at all. I don't believe in all those stories."

"I'm just relaying the message, not asking you to become religious."

Now I wanted to leave, but I wanted to be gentle about it. She was so calm and peaceful, and you just can't be rude to a person like that.

"What does the story say?" I asked.

"I don't know. All I know is that your mother wanted you to check the Koran she used to read every day. There's a note with her handwriting that will explain the story of Zachary."

She went on to explain how I should not avoid my emotions but rather feel the pain of my mother's passing and how I should have faith in the self-discovery path I'd recently undertaken, which would be long but meaningful if I stayed true to it. If I had complete faith in myself and my new beliefs, then I would keep walking toward my true self, she said, looking straight at me.

I felt a rush of hope inside of me. It was as if someone, perhaps my mother, had my back. I wasn't alone anymore. The world, the universe was with me.

On the way back to my father's home, I googled the story of Zachary. He was prominent in both the Bible and the Koran. Zachary had unwavering faith in God and would pray to Him incessantly. He and his wife were very old, and the time for them to conceive a child had passed. But Zachary desired a son to continue the prophethood. God responded to his faith immediately by granting Zachary a son—John. This was no ordinary child; God created John righteous, wise, compassionate, and free from sin.

Later that day, I asked my dad for my mother's Koran, the one she had read diligently every morning for as long as I could remember. I opened it and carefully turned the pages. Right in the middle I saw a note folded in four. I opened it.

It was in Arabic and challenging for me to read, but I could easily make out the name—Zachary. My heart skipped a beat. Wasn't that what the faith healer told me? My face went white as the blood quickly rushed elsewhere, prepping me to flee. I was shocked, confused, and afraid. First, the faith healer had predicted that my mother's favourite passage in the Koran mentioned Zachary. Secondly, my mother always had a problem with my siblings and me not believing and having any faith in the "Unseen," instead always focusing on evidence and perception.

I didn't dare mention it to anyone. Not even to my sister. I just made up a few stories and explained to her that it was a good experience. How could I explain the unexplainable? My mother was clearly telling me to have more faith in God, more faith in the world, and more faith in myself.

August was now coming to an end. My father had moved to his new home, and it was time to say our farewells. We all met up one final time at my father's house and stayed there for a few nights. We were all going back to our separate lives. My sister went back to Kuwait and remained heartbroken. Out of all of us, she was the most devastated and just couldn't reconcile the suddenness of my mother's death.

Back in Ghana, all things were now returning to normal. After the double shock of the summer, I had to get my life back in order. Andrus's death was like a wakeup call to life's fragility, whereas my mother's death had a deeper effect on me, one that pushed me to hide under the shield I'd constructed during my school days. Looking back now, I'd say I lost a lot of my vulnerability gains then. I didn't want to process her death much, and I'd inadvertently raised the wall again around my heart. I did what I always do well, getting on with my life, allowing my routines to take over, and abandoning the clarity of thought I'd had when I journaled after Andrus's death.

But my body had other plans. One Saturday morning soon after my return, I finished a ten-kilometre run and was feeling on top of the world. I sat outside in the open air facing the pool. The trees were swaying, the birds were singing, and I was just about to start my daily poetry writing. Then suddenly, pain hit me hard in my stomach, and I was hit with wave after wave of feverish attacks. I knew these were not the usual fever symptoms. The pain got worse, and it was like nothing I had felt before. Nausea, stomach upset, pounding heart, cold sweat, trembling body, and dizziness. Those were the physical symptoms, and hard as they were, I could handle them.

The mental symptoms that followed were the ones that shattered me. I got a severe, miserable feeling, which made me helpless, lifeless, and surrounded by nothingness. This all-sinking feeling was like being in the deep, dark abyss of a well. I couldn't get out or even see any possibility of doing so. I just lay on the floor, curled up, and felt worthless. The birds that were singing had left; the trees that were swaying now became stationary, lifeless objects.

This feeling lasted for eons and eons and not the real five minutes that it took. I didn't know what was happening and felt confused and paralysed. All I could think of was jumping off a cliff or a tall skyscraper, but luckily the closest places like that were hundreds of miles away. I tried to think through what was happening, but when I did, it was as if an irritable fly were inside my mind, buzzing away in every corner, and there were no windows that I could open to let it out.

Now I know that it was a hypoglycaemic attack. This is when there is not enough sugar in the bloodstream. The first area to be affected is the brain, as it doesn't store any glucose and is totally dependent on the amount of sugar in the bloodstream. The brain, starved of energy, then starts reacting badly, causing those severe symptoms. I'd been diagnosed with hypoglycaemia a few years back when I upped my running regimen. Since then, I had regulated my diet and thought I had reversed it. But now I was sure it was an attack—and the most severe I'd ever gone through.

My anxiety and thoughts were spiralling, and my initial fears of blacking out transformed into the conviction that I was going to die right then. I staggered up to my room and lay on the floor. The house was empty since my wife and kids were out. The fear compounded the pain, and confusion was taking me to my darkest parts. I was now picturing how my teenage kids would survive without me. I was angry at the universe, as I still had many things to do, many things to be. I was also furious that I was going to die now after all the good work I had done for myself, after all the ladders I had climbed, after the sweet spot I had found for myself following the torment of summer.

But here I was, helpless, and I couldn't lift my head, let alone change my attitude. I felt sorry for myself and wanted a break. What was the universe throwing at me in that moment? What was the lesson?

I just stayed on the floor and cried and prayed hard. The faith healer and my mother's advice on having faith quickly flooded in. I clung to a new mantra that I'd started to use: "This too shall pass." It's not very sophisticated, but it usually works. Slowly a bit of hope started penetrating my mind.

Then, my daughter, who had just come home, rushed toward me. I got up. Noticing that something was wrong with me, she hugged me. I held onto her for a few seconds, and suddenly hope broke through the mind-vaulted gates of my heart like a tidal wave crushing all the doubts, fears, and negative thoughts that had engulfed me just a moment before.

I explained to my daughter what had happened and told her to get me orange juice and that I'd rest alone in my room. I lay in bed, and my shoulders, so hard and tense, started to soften as I slowly relaxed and felt the gaps in between my anxious and fearful thinking widen. I got more intentional with my thoughts, put on some meditative music, and started breathing in and out. I followed that by chanting my mantra of "This too shall pass" for some minutes. I got a hold of myself—my true self.

As always, it was my body that kept the score. It was reminding me that it was not okay to repress my grief. Yes, I hadn't eaten enough, and I'd been running, which made my calorie output exceed my calorie intake. But this was no ordinary attack. It seemed that my body was not going to let me off the hook again. I had to express myself, no matter how dark the emotions were. The samskaras would not be allowed to form as easily as before.

The end of 2015 came, and sitting down to review it was a Herculean task. It had been a tumultuous year full of contrasting highs—visiting Gibran's mausoleum, attending the Tony Robbins event, my TEDx Talk—and the lows of both Andrus's and my mother's deaths along with the inexplicable hypoglycaemia attacks I suffered.

I'd vowed to lead a simpler life, one that would make me more attuned to my goals, but somehow life got in the way, which meant that all those promises just faded away.

I still couldn't rationalise the events of the faith healer no matter how much I tried. I wanted to have more faith in myself, the world, and God. But how could I move beyond just accepting it as a concept to living it day to day? I had tried a gratitude diary, which didn't work well for me. Following the strict procedures of religion also didn't do it for me. Maybe, as always, I was overthinking this.

Looking back at my successes over the past years, there was a common theme. Whether it was changing my company's vision to focus on quality and service instead of just plain numbers, acknowledging this burning passion inside of me to write, deciding to start running at age forty-six—and completing a half marathon six months later—or sharing my thoughts on self-discovery with TEDx and finding myself on stage within a few months, my decisions were based not on logic but rather on intuition and the unwavering faith that I could accomplish them. I had inadvertently pushed aside my egoic, thinking mind and relied on instinct and faith instead. I had acted as if driven by some outside force.

Maybe my mother was trying to tell me it was time to have more faith in my life. More faith in myself. More faith in a supreme being. It was time to be humble enough to surrender to life and be more accepting. To live my ideologies whole-heartedly. To allow myself to have faith in the power of the unseen—the invisible. To let go of my self-imposed shackles that required everything to have a logical explanation.

She was telling me that the best way to find out if I could trust life and a supreme power was *to trust them*. Perhaps she was also telling me that, in the same way I should trust life, I must also trust death. That death was also part of life. That maybe her death would not be the last I saw or heard from her. And that maybe it was time I started to process her death, to let my shield down and feel the pain and sadness I had to feel. Trust the process of grief. Perhaps there was a deeper and more spiritual shift I needed to make. I was learning to surrender, painful though it was, and that too was a kind of growth.

Chapter 8

Reclaiming My Authenticity

I spent the Christmas of 2015 in Bali with my entire nuclear family. The trip was organised by Imman. She wanted us to spend the holidays with my father after my mother's passing—but not in Lebanon. It was a wonderful idea and one of the few times where all four siblings, with spouses and children, would meet.

Since moving south to the town he grew up in, my father had been surrounded by his family, who numbered in the hundreds. I was never close to his extended family because of growing up in Ghana and England. They were extremely religious, parochial, non-Western oriented, and so different to my way of thinking. Perhaps that's why my mother had resisted moving there.

Though my father became more embedded in Islam and its customs, he remained open-minded and accepting to all ways. True, he was a man of faith, committed to and at harmony with Islam. But he was not a blind follower, instead an avid reader of Islamic history and philosophy. Though fundamentalists and politics have hijacked Islam, he keeps reminding us that "Islam" not only means *surrender* but also shares roots with an Arabic word, "Salam," which means *peace*.

His incredible love for life and people meant that he recovered from being a widower within months and started to build a new life. Back in his town, he became the de facto chieftain of his community. His house was never empty, and he often hosted many lunches and dinners, where he would reach out to his tribe by inspiring the younger ones to broaden their thinking and helping them solve many of their issues. One story I heard from a relative was how he'd supported a young member of the family who was always in trouble. This boy was involved in drugs and theft and had even burgled my father's home once. When the entire family gave up on him, my dad refused to do so. He helped in his rehabilitation and offered him support. In short, he gave him love and acceptance—something no other person had—and that helped him become a reformed character.

Listening to how he'd acclimated to his new environment and learning of the humility with which he served as a leader was another reminder to me on how to counterbalance striving with serving. It was that faith in life and humanity that my mother had been asking me to find through the faith healer I'd seen after she passed. It was that faith that would lead to the inner peace and satisfaction that I longed for. Perhaps for me that faith did not need to be through religion but instead through the knowledge that I was part of life's formula—a non-dogmatic spirituality where there was a supreme intelligence who organised the world and through which I could tap into the divine.

The Bali trip was meant to make us bond, relax, and celebrate our mother. Instead, I'd spent it in a foul mood, arguing with Imman over petty things like which restaurant to go to or whether to visit the elephant safari or the monkey palace and whether we would celebrate New Year's Eve at the hotel or go somewhere else.

These trivial arguments masked what was truly going on. My sister, in her grief, needed emotional support from her brother while I, with my shield up, had become oblivious to her needs.

The holiday ended, and our issues were never resolved. I just couldn't handle any emotional turbulence at the time. Maybe that was my way of grieving too. I'd offer myself physically, but emotionally I'd be absent. I knew it wasn't right, but I just couldn't give more.

Growing up with three siblings who were much older than I was meant that I grew up as a loner and wasn't good in larger groups. I'd learn later that being an introvert meant that I needed solitude and pockets of alone time to recharge my batteries before I could reflect on my behaviour and get back into the stir of life.

The rest of my family had flown to Bali from Lebanon, but I'd come from a business meeting in Dubai. Since we then left on different flights, I decided to stay by myself for two extra nights. It was Bali after all, and after the tumultuous last six months and my grouchiness with the family, it was a perfect place where I could rejuvenate and find some inner peace to reflect. How could I become authentic if I didn't rid myself of my demons first?

The next morning, I sent Imman an email apologising for my behaviour and vowing to have a longer conversation with her when I got back home.

Inspired by Rolf Potts's book, *Vagabonding*, on how to travel and explore countries in a non-touristic and more soulful way, I rented a moped to discover Bali. With the wind blowing across my face, I sped up the narrow meandering roads of a sprawling town called Seminyak in Bali, feeling free, exhilarated, and like an intrepid traveller exploring the island. I then left Seminyak and drove toward the surfing town of Kuta.

I was on the way to meet a yoga guru who would teach me a few insights. I had planned to explore yoga after reading and listening to the incessant information now flowing into the world about its benefits. The instructor's story was interesting; he had left his high-strung corporate job to learn surfing in Bali. It was so cheap that he'd lived off his savings for many years. Along with surfing, he started to learn yoga on the island, and slowly he found his peace and vocation by becoming a yoga instructor. He had simplified his life. He surfed during the day, watched sunsets, and connected spiritually through yoga. He had no responsibilities perched on his shoulders. No wife as he was divorced, no kids as they were with her, and no shackles from working a nine-to-five job.

He did show me a few good yoga moves and explained how they would be good for my mobility, but what I mostly took from our meeting was the beaming smile on his face. It was the look of contentment. I yearned for that smile of freedom, for that peace, and for finding my authentic core but was helpless as to where to start.

In the time I had left in Bali, I wanted to explore how I could start to reclaim my authenticity. So next I visited Ubud, the spiritual haven of Bali. Unfortunately, I found it to be typically touristic, filled with small shops selling incense, crystals, and the like. There was nothing spiritual about it, and the humidity and heat didn't help. Perhaps the vagabonding kind of travelling I craved was nothing but an escape from my real life. I likely didn't find the elixir of life on those two days by myself, but I did feel rejuvenated and ready to go back home.

Back in Ghana, the same old frustrations were eating me up. I closed the latest self-help book I was reading. Sure, it gave me great joy in understanding its central message, but there was a lingering voice in me telling me to burn all my self-help books. To go out and live life instead!

I'd based my life on learning and reading, and I knew how central they had been to my growth. However, it was time to start experiencing much more of life. There should be a balance in our lives, a time to read the books and a time to go out and live. There is cowardice and comfort in reading and learning without daring greatly, and there is shallowness in living a completely sensual, experiential life.

Luckily, I found the right book at the right time—Nikos Kazantzakis's famous novel *Zorba the Greek*, which until today ranks as one of the best books that I've ever read. In it, Zorba is this larger-than-life character who is passionate, fearless, and always lives in the moment. He is illiterate yet ingenious and profoundly more philosophical in his daily activities than any book or self-help guru could be. I cut a quote from the book and pasted it on a wall facing my home desk:

"I should learn to run, to wrestle, to swim, to ride horses, to row, to drive a car, to fire a rifle. I should fill my soul with flesh. I should fill my flesh with soul. In fact, I should reconcile at last within me the two internal antagonists."

How could I live a life of reflection *and* of action? How could I go out and live more mindfully and not remain rooted in rumination and procrastination?

These were the questions that were troubling me now. Zorba had some answers. Free of social conventions, he lives life to its fullest with passion and without expectations. He embodies living a life with a deep feeling of awe, gratitude, and wonder. For him, life is for living and for experiencing sensual joy; he is the antithesis of the learned and the scholarly and rails against the "pen pushers." He strips himself of his inhibitions and allows his heart to lead him to the mysteries of life. He recognises that he cannot live life through his mind but rather allows life to live through him.

Life was happening right now, and I was missing it because I was stuck in regretting the past or thinking of how I could make the future better. The present moment is where our true essence lies and where eternal brilliance prevails. Zorba's day starts afresh without the spectre of what happened yesterday. He holds onto memories as treasures, hoping to share them with friends, and talks about his dreams as if they are inspiring him rather than holding him back. He cries when he is sad, laughs when happy, and works hard when he has to put food on the table. He plays the santuri and sings when his heart so desires. He lives entirely in the present.

Our ultimate goal as human beings is to be free, yet we allow ourselves to cling to every form of enslavement possible. Whether it's to material things, conforming to society, living in our comfort zone, or seeking the extraordinary all the time, we find ourselves stuck. Our greatest triumph would be to free ourselves completely and go back to our childhood days when we were free of anxiety, guilt, fear, and worry. We were born free, and it's to that state we must return. Could I remove the shackles that held me back? The demons that would come up every now and then, like my quarrel with Imman?

Inspired by Zorba and a new tattoo on my left forearm that read "Be Here Now," I recognised that the only way to remove demons is to act and live more in the present. I lined up several talks with reclaiming our authenticity as the central message. The first one was for teachers, administrators, and staff at the Lincoln community school my children had attended and where I also served as a trustee. I repeated my TED Talk but this time with much more intensity and focus on authenticity. To date, I've never received a better reception or felt such humility after a talk. I don't know if it was that people in education got my message more than others or if I was truly inspirational that day, but every time I recall the reception and the number of people who later came up or wrote to me, I tear up in awe.

With Ella's encouragement and support, I also started to teach a twelve-week self-help programme to a group of ladies from our Lebanese community. I titled the programme "The Shift," and that would later become the raw material for my first book. In these talks, I was not only sharing principles but seeing how they could work in real life. I was guiding the women through steps on the how-to rather than just on the philosophical why and what.

In May, I started an initiative called The Authenticity Project (TAP). My idea for the project was to celebrate those people who were living authentic and inspiring lives in order to encourage others, especially myself, to follow what their hearts truly wanted. At the launch party, I delivered the following speech:

> "Authenticity comes from the Latin word *author* and simply means to become the author of one's life. Being authentic means coming from a real place within, where our actions and words are congruent with our beliefs and values. Authenticity is not a destination but a journey of deep self-discovery. It requires self-knowledge and self-awareness.
>
> "Living authentically is not stagnant. It is constantly shifting and taking on new forms, and we must continually be learning about ourselves, challenging old beliefs, facing our fears, and

courageously reaching deep within ourselves to find out what makes our hearts sing and our spirits soar. True authenticity is being ourselves and not an imitation of what we think we should be or what others want us to be. We all have a unique gift or talent, and we must find it and nurture it as it will give us the greatest platform to become who we must be and as such serve humanity accordingly."

In the self-help world, it's commonly said that "success leaves clues." As such, I wanted to profile people who had done it and made a difference in Ghana. In June of 2016, I drove for two hours along impassable roads to interview Patrick Awuah, who rather serendipitously was the first person to have congratulated me after my TEDx Talk. He was also the founder and president of the remarkable Ashesi University and had previously worked as an engineer at Microsoft before quitting to start the university.

At first, Awuah encountered many problems, not least from the many existing, more traditional competing universities that disliked his new ideology on education. However, he had faith and persevered in his project, and within a few months, feedback from the parents of the school's students was fantastic. They felt their children were transformed into self-confident, mature leaders rather than just knowledgeable students. He went on to receive the MacArthur Fellowship for his work in 2015 and in the same year was named among the world's fifty greatest leaders by *Fortune Magazine*.

Today, Awuah's work provides a model for the whole of Africa on how to set up a viable university that can produce great leaders at a reasonable cost. Many top educators from all over the world come to visit the campus to see how they can best replicate his creation.

The Authenticity Project profiled Awuah's story as an aspirational one. However, I wanted to hear more stories from people living authentically. Ones that were not as famous or successful as Awuah but nevertheless made a difference to their communities. There were many people who were either unknown or were reluctant to reveal their inspiring life stories. The initiative was aimed at encouraging such people to come forward and share.

I hoped to select and highlight some of the most authentic stories submitted to us at an event to be held in May of 2017. There, a small panel of five people, mainly people I had met through TEDx, would identify one winner. The winner would then receive a cash prize and a one-year mentorship programme from a selection of our inspiring TAP ambassadors. It was an emboldening project and one that gave me a great sense of purpose.

I was now doing the things that excited me and that brought me to life. However, I couldn't forget how writing made my heart dance and wanted it to play a bigger part in my life. I chanced on a writing course in Paris on one of my favourite podcasts—The Tim Ferriss Show. Ferriss was interviewing Rolf Potts, who wrote *Vagabonding* and inspired Ferriss to take off to Buenos Aires and write the much-acclaimed book, *The 4-Hour Workweek*. In the interview, Potts mentioned that he offered a mini-MFA writing course in Paris.

I had just finished reading Hemingway's *A Moveable Feast*, which describes Hemingway's life during the roaring twenties in Paris with the other artists from the lost generation. I quickly signed up for the writing retreat and was eager to travel to Paris and immerse myself in the writing world for a month.

The one-month course in Paris also offered me the opportunity to live alone in a rented Airbnb flat in the Latin Quarters of Paris. Writing was not the only thing I was about to learn. I had never lived alone before and had hardly done any household chores. The truth was that I'd always lived a privileged life. Growing up in England, my mother and some hired help did most of the chores. In Ghana, it was the norm that every household had several maids, a driver, and a cook. Over the next few weeks, I was embarrassed to find out that I couldn't do simple things like wash my clothes or prepare my own food, but learn I did. I'd wash my clothes, clean the bathroom, iron my shirts and trousers, and sometimes prepare light dinners. It was all part of my authenticity education.

On the first morning of the course, I arrived at the Paris American Academy only to be flabbergasted to find that Tim Ferriss, one of my current heroes and host of a podcast I'd listened to throughout 2016, was also enrolled in the writing course. In *The Alchemist*, Paulo Coelho wrote, "When you want something, all the universe conspires in helping you to achieve it." I guess I had wanted to meet Tim Ferriss.

He had come over to Paris to meet with his friend Potts and get inspired as he was writing his latest book. He spent a few classes with us, and on one occasion, he offered us a free Q&A session to ask him anything we wanted.

What I took out of my chance meeting was that, although I revered him, Tim Ferriss was just a normal person. He was driven, successful, and focused, that much was clear, but he was also very much human. He was much shorter than I expected, didn't have the presence I'd thought he'd have, and had an annoying way of being too prepared, almost contrived. He wasn't natural. He wasn't free. He wasn't as at peace with himself as others who I'd met. This is no slight on Ferriss—he helped me tremendously in my own growth and has helped millions of others—but rather on my fixation on ambition and habit of idolising people for the wrong reasons.

Living on my own and in Paris of all places was like the authentic me being unleashed. I had no work, no family, and no responsibilities. I was released from all kinds of decision making. I was solely immersed in my passion for writing in the most romantic city of all. I quickly made some friends who were of different ages and backgrounds. I also enjoyed lectures that gave me a taste of all writing forms—poetry, fiction, non-fiction, and screenplay. We were given much to read and some writing homework. At age forty-eight, I felt like a twenty-year-old again, back in university.

Though I was immersed in the writing world, the writing didn't become easier. A week into the course, I had an assignment deadline and found myself stuck. With only a day to go to my deadline, I hadn't written a single word yet, and I had no clue where to start. Writers surrounded me: teachers, colleagues, and weird people in cafes. I was in Paris for God's sake! This was where everyone got inspired to write. I was away from the stress of my business and the mundanity of my life. The environment was perfect for writing.

Finally, I took a break from staring at the blank computer screen to get some fresh air and decided to take a walk to clear my thoughts though I didn't know where I was going. The sun set late in the Parisian summers, and the long days made walking not just appealing but also soul-nourishing. I decided that there would be no writing that day, and the thought freed me.

I wandered through the streets of Paris like a true flaneur—a term coined by Charles Baudelaire. It means to saunter through the city aimlessly, experiencing it through our senses, removing ourselves from the world, and putting ourselves into the heart of a city to become one with it. I suddenly found myself in front of the Jardin du Luxembourg. The gardens were spread over many acres. All kinds of flowers bloomed in different colours, offering differing scents that urged creativity whenever I breathed. People laughed, children played, and lovers kissed. Most of all I saw and felt life, and it was everywhere. No one seemed to care that I couldn't write.

I was astonished how history found me on every road, nook, and alley of this city. I found myself outside the University of Paris-Sorbonne, where Victor Hugo and many other notable figures attended university. I took a right at the end of the Pantheon and walked for a while to find myself in Place de la Contrescarpe. I was in front of a Patisserie Pascal Pinaud, and a strawberry tart jumped out at me. I sat down for a coffee and the sugar that I craved. On my right, an old lady was reading an English book. She looked up and smiled at me. I asked her if this was the area that Hemingway frequented, and she pointed to a plaque approximately twenty metres away, which showed where Hemingway lived with Hadley, his first wife, when they moved to Paris.

I recalled how one day my son asked me what had spurred my sudden passion for writing. Was it out of loneliness? Perhaps. But maybe I had finally reached a time when I couldn't bottle up any more of my thoughts, feelings, and words. They had to come out. I had lived most of my life pursuing success, money, and prestige. I had been like a robot using only my mind to keep my feet firmly on the material side of life while ignoring my heart. Writing seemed to have been something that lay dormant in me; it was hidden deep in the crevasses of my heart, waiting to explode like a wild volcanic eruption.

Writing transformed me emotionally, releasing much of what had held me back since childhood. I had started to finally align my feelings and actions. The more I did that, the freer I felt and the closer I got to my true self. I was also getting farther away from my old inauthentic ways of living.

I turned around to say goodbye to the old woman, but she had left. I got up and noticed a vendor wearing dark trousers and a navy-blue shirt with a short apron on top. He was beaming, and his smile was not only inviting but exuded joy. He talked in rapid French to a couple of locals, and I couldn't understand a word. He held a purple aubergine in his hands, and I imagined he was explaining how fresh it was (having just received his consignment only a few hours ago) and how best to cook it. He did this with such passion that I wanted to buy the aubergine myself, even though I wouldn't know what to do with it. I just kept watching him for a while as he connected with people. He obviously loved what he was doing.

I was envious—I wanted to be free enough to get lost in the present moment. I wondered if writing truly could become the platform that would make me feel authentic to myself, where I could finally lose my analytical thoughts and become more present. Carl Jung wrote, "The privilege of a lifetime is to become who you truly are." I wanted, through writing, to finally become the true me.

Chapter 9

Making the Shift

If 2016 was the year where I began to understand the concept of authenticity, then 2017 was the year that I realised writing was one path for me to reclaim it. I wanted to explore the writing world like never before.

Having finished a small poetry book, I intended to self-publish and have it out within the next three months. Even though I felt that my poetry was not something to be proud of in terms of literary quality, I wanted to get it out in the world and off my chest. The poems revealed a lot about my struggle to balance my two ways of being: a hard-nosed, conventional businessman versus a calmer, more accepting, spiritual, and creative being. Only years later did I realise it didn't have to be an either/or.

I also wanted to prove to myself and to the people around me that I was a good writer, one who was not frittering away his time on some romantic pursuit. The title of the book was serious and mysterious: *The Dense Mistiness of the Ordinary.*

After the book came out, though, I never did behave as if I considered myself a serious writer. I didn't have the courage to promote the book or even try to sell it. I just gave it away for free to my friends and anyone who was interested.

Looking back now, the writing was not as bad as I'd thought; my lack of confidence in my ability as a writer was the real issue. It was rather surprising as I'd always been confident in myself, whether that was in business, sports, or being among people. When it came to writing, however, I was always one negative comment away from feeling like an imposter. It was as if I were a fake writer who had self-published because no one else would publish my work. I felt like I was in a world where I didn't belong, even though, for the past three years, I'd blogged consistently with many articles going viral and receiving much positive feedback from readers.

At the start of the year, I applied and was accepted for a two-year MFA programme in writing non-fiction at Goddard College in Vermont. I hoped the programme would build my confidence as a writer. I was both excited and anxious about both the programme and my impending travels to Vermont for a one-week residency in June. Before all that, I wanted to complete a non-fiction self-help book that encompassed all the learnings I'd been through over the past ten years.

Most of what would end up in the book would come from the "Shift" course that I'd given to a group of Lebanese ladies during 2016. The twelve-week programme I taught them included topics such as the growth mindset, taming the ego, the power of vulnerability, how to know thyself, and emotional intelligence. All the things that I'd learned over the years and had applied in my life.

Every week, we'd go through one topic and end with how we could apply more of it in our lives. In "know thyself," I had them go through many online questionnaires to understand who they were, their strengths and values and what things they were interested in, so that they could perhaps take steps toward the things they enjoyed. I did help some of them shift their lives in the directions they wanted. At the same time, the programme also helped me greatly in that I now knew the lessons well enough and became more accountable in practicing them.

Though I had my notes, thoughts, and ideas on how to write the book, I still needed to sit down and do it. I wanted to finish it before my impending travels to Goddard College in June. However, it was now March, and I still hadn't written a word.

The procrastination was not circumstantial but was deeper, masked by the many fears lying in my subconscious. During those arid writing months, I'd get my laptop out and proceed to spend the next few hours doing nothing but staring at the blank screen, followed by much ruminating on why I couldn't write. The truth was I shouldn't have worried whether I wrote or not. My livelihood didn't depend on writing. I was not contracted by any newspaper or beholden to any pressing deadline. I had no expected date of manuscript submission to an editor. I was self-publishing a book for *me*. Yet during those few months of not writing, I ended each day full of guilt. I had linked my new authentic self's worth to writing. Thus, in not writing, I'd become nothing.

Finally, a week into March, I decided that I needed to do something about my lack of writing. What was the source of the procrastination? Why had I felt so bad when I stopped writing? Using some ideas from Julia Cameron again, I first gave myself permission not to write for a whole week. Then I wrote in bold letters on an index card, "Why do I feel that I must create?" and carried it with me for a week.

As is always the case when we focus our consciousness on a particular question or incident, many answers serendipitously arose—thoughts, conversations, articles, movies, books, and more. I came across a simple but telling contribution from one of my favourite writers, poets and thinkers, Khalil Gibran. In a letter to Mary Haskell penned on November 10, 1911, Gibran wrote:

> "There is an old Arabic song which begins 'Only God and I know what is in my heart'—and today, after rereading your last three letters, I said out loud, 'Only God and Mary and I know what is in my heart.' I would open my heart and carry it in my hand so that others may know also; for there is no deeper desire than the desire of being revealed. We all want that little light in us to be taken from under the bushel. The first poet must have suffered

much when the cave-dwellers laughed at his mad words. He would have given his bow and arrows and lion skin, everything he possessed, just to have his fellow men know the delight and the passion which the sunset had created in his soul. And yet, is it not this mystic pain—the pain of not being known—that gives birth to art and artists?"

Gibran's words are so elegant that his wisdom never fails to strike me instantaneously. "There is no deeper desire than the desire of being revealed." I meditated on that sentence for a while and realised that, like all human beings, I yearned to reveal my true inner self to the outside world. I wanted my madness to be seen. To be accepted. To be understood.

Creativity and writing were the driving force that helped me find my inner voice, the means through which I share my authentic self with the world. Through exposing my writing to public audiences I've learned I'm part of an interconnected whole. However, even though we are all connected, we are also unique beings. As such, I felt a compulsive longing to show my individuality with writing. Just like a peacock is proud to display his colourful array of feathers, we naturally do the same. It is an aspect of our evolutionary psychology. There is no ego or shame. "This is who I am," we say.

Little wonder then that my writing stalled. There was a lot at stake for me. I was afraid to reveal my inner core to the world, thinking that most readers would judge me as not being good enough. The three-month timeline also didn't help as I put undue pressure on myself.

But with Gibran's definition of creativity and the understanding I got from why I was writing, the shackles came off. I was writing the best book I could, the one that only I could write. Perhaps I was no Yeats or Hemingway, but I was me. The poetry book was good enough for me. The self-help book was good enough for me. That was all that mattered. I could only show off the feathers that were unique to me.

With that in mind, I finally sat down to write. I created a plan that would help me effectively write and complete my book over the next ninety days.

I needed to focus and find a way to put aside all the distractions. I had to summon the powers of intense focus that all the great writers seem to have, but like most people today, I was an internet/social media/email addict. I craved the dopamine hit that came from my smartphone or laptop. So, I removed all social media applications and email from my phone. I set some time in the late afternoon to check email, surf the net, and look at my social media accounts—but not during the time I had allotted to write my book.

Establishing these rituals made it easier to initiate and maintain focus. For my actual writing sessions, I started with an espresso, put on my noise-cancelling headphones to listen to classical music, and then started typing. I aimed for three sessions of uninterrupted forty-minute slots per writing day with five-minute breaks in between. During breaks, I walked around, stretched, and made another coffee. I wrote on Mondays, Wednesdays, Saturdays, and Sundays and left the other days writing-free to focus on my work.

I also tracked my progress on a calendar with a simple cross when I completed a writing session. I hung the calendar over my writing desk, and as I made progress and connected the crosses, marking the hours of work I did per week, I felt encouraged and more confident about completing my book.

I finished my first draft within two months. The final month, I worked on rewriting. Finally, at the end of May, I sent my final draft off to an editor I'd met through my writing for *Elephant Journal*. I was now free to enjoy my daughter's weeklong graduation celebrations and was able to be there for her with a great sense of relief and joy that comes when one completes a manuscript.

The one-week stay at the Vermont college was now coming up fast. My writing MFA programme and travel to the States piqued a lot of interest from my friends and family. My wife, children, and a few good friends were enthusiastic and happy for me as they'd been throughout my authenticity journey. They were the ones who always reassured me.

However, I did feel some judgement and cynicism from the wider society. I recall how one of my friends informed me that other friends had ridiculed me. Although she had defended me by pointing out how nice it was to see someone doing what he loved, it still hurt to know people I considered friends were mocking my efforts. Every snide comment I received added to my imposter syndrome because I hadn't yet begun to see myself as a writer.

I arrived in Vermont just after midnight. The drive to Goddard College in Plainfield was nearly an hour long, and it was raining incessantly. There were few towns along the way, and it felt like the campus was in the middle of nowhere. I finally reached a collection of buildings spread out over many acres. This was going to be my home for the next eight days. I got out of the cab, lugged my bags through the rain, and entered an office where I found the students' check-in desk. I was then directed to the Fitzpatrick Quarters, where I found my room.

I had forgotten how small school dormitory rooms could be. The communal bathroom had three toilets, two washbasins, and two showers, all housed in a single space smaller than my bathroom at home. I had been telling myself that I was yearning for the simplicity of a backpacker's life. But that first night—and the thought of sharing a bathroom with six others—quickly quashed my dreams. Maybe that basic life wasn't exactly for me. It seemed that luxury and creature comforts had become indelibly marked on my being. Yet the next eight days of living like a twenty-year-old student not only proved to be some of the best days I'd had for a long time but also made me feel so much more deeply alive.

The week I spent at the writing college took me back to the nostalgic days of my youth. True, the bed was hard, the pillow was awful, and sharing a bathroom was awkward, but all these supposed hardships paled in comparison to the lightness, freedom, and sense of community that I gained from the minimalistic way of life on campus. I felt like I was stripped naked to the authentic me. The simplicity of removing too many layers of luxury brought my sensory feelings back to life.

The teachers at Goddard were all current writers who taught part-time in this residency format. In this programme, we would be in Vermont one week every six months for two years while the rest of our learning was done online. The professors were friendly, encouraging us to share our work and to embrace critiquing. At first, I feared sharing my writing and awaiting the communal critique. However, I quickly warmed to it as the tough love approach suited my character—though I found it easier to accept criticism than to give it, unlike many others there.

The tutors assigned us a book a week to read, annotate, and study. We would also have to write longer critical papers and finally, by the end of the programme, a book. Before we went back, we were expected to choose the books we would read over the next six months and decide on the book we wanted to write.

The first few days of the programme, I was overawed. Not only were most students younger than I was, but I was also one of the few non-Americans. It was as if I had been transported back to my first few weeks of school in England when I had just arrived from Ghana and all the eyes were on me. I was stunned by how quickly that feeling of not being one of the "people" came up. With my still festering imposter syndrome, I lacked so much confidence that I was shy and kept to myself, a far cry from who I truly was. I'd sit at lunches and dinners with the group I was assigned to, listening to them speak in literary language, using American slang, talking about current affairs that I wasn't aware of, and feel inadequate. I was also finding it hard to follow all the information and technical instructions given out by the teachers.

After a few days of feeling inferior, I took an afternoon off to recalibrate myself. All the self-help work and journaling I'd done meant that I knew what to do when things felt off. I reminded myself of who I was, the experiences that I'd had, and that I was in no way lesser than anyone. True, many seemed to have better writing skills, but writing was a craft at the end of the day and could be learned. However, who I was and the ideas in my head were unique to me.

On that afternoon, I completed my first assignment—a Flannery O'Connor short story. That evening, I read one of my spiritual-based articles aloud to the group and felt that I'd finally arrived at the MFA course. The next day, I sent out my carefully selected list of literary books to read and chose a memoir about the last ten years of my life and my ever-growing shift to authenticity as my thesis—the book you're reading now.

I got back to Ghana and quickly forgot my minimalistic experience as I stepped into the comfort that was entrenched in my life. One week of austerity, though soul nourishing, was not going to erase years of building a life around luxury. It was the life of convenience that I'd built over time that made it difficult for me to transform instantly into living more simply. However, at least now I was more aware and wanted to make some changes both at work and at home to accommodate my new way of thinking.

It was now September and, with no writing assignments until October, it was time for my second trip to the States. I hadn't been to the States since I was a kid, and now I was at JFK Airport for the second time in two months. This time around, my daughter was going to college. Together with my wife and Nader, we were all on our way to Savannah, Georgia to enrol my daughter into Savannah College of Art and Design (SCAD). It was rather ironic that my daughter's name was also Savannah, something that didn't fail to amuse many locals.

Before that big event, we would first spend a week in New York. I was immediately entranced by and enamoured with Manhattan and its skyscrapers. The energy of the city was amazing. True, I was only there on holiday, but still the buzz and the constant movement completely contrasted with Accra. Perhaps, I wouldn't be able to handle such energy for too long, but nevertheless I enjoyed the novelty and excitement.

One morning, I was walking down Thompson Street in Soho when a hat shop caught my eye. I went in, and within minutes, I was wearing a greyish black beret. I don't know why, but I had always subconsciously associated a beret with writers. It wasn't like what Che Guevara wore in his iconic pictures, but somehow it made me feel revolutionary.

I walked for hours that morning with the beret on my head, and no one even looked at me. I felt light, different, and most of all I felt a sense of freedom in my veins, as if this was how the new "Mo" was going to be. There was no imposter syndrome. I felt like a writer and not a businessman trying to be a writer. The adage that you can be anyone or do anything in New York and no one would care came as a welcome relief from the parochial life I lived back in Ghana. There, every move I made was scrutinised and subjected to judgement by friends, family, and my history. For a brief minute I felt as if I'd worn that same beret in another life and that I was more connected to the peasant writer I once was.

After hurricane Irma forced us to stay an extra week in New York, we finally made it to the picturesque town that was Savannah.

"Why did you decide to call your daughter Savannah?" asked a cheerful volunteer showing us around SCAD.

Interesting question. I had no answer. I only recalled that the name came to me suddenly, and my wife smiled and nodded her approval on the hospital bed.

I had no connection to or history with Savannah. The funny part was that the town itself was very much like Accra, where my daughter was brought up. That September, it was hot and humid in Savannah. There were not many tall buildings, but rather the geography was dominated by smaller houses and buildings. It also had a cosy, small-town feeling to it, one that my daughter would quickly acclimate to.

On my last day in Savannah, I walked my daughter to her new dorm room and then walked back again alone to the hotel, crying my eyes out and having one thought in my mind. How did eighteen years pass so quickly? It was similar to the walk I'd had when I dropped my son off at the train station in England when he went to university almost three years before.

My trip to the States helped me to feel more like a writer, but I was about to get an even bigger boost. By mid-October, I received the first published copy of my book *The Shift*. I had self-published, and the process from finishing the manuscript to having a copy in my hand was fast. I looked at the cover of my book and was proud of my efforts. All those learnings and writing hours condensed into the palm of my hand.

I arranged a small event to launch the book. I didn't want any grand events anymore. It was as if I didn't want to poison the literary part of my life with the grandness I lived in my normal life. I was keeping things simple. That was one change I could implement immediately.

However, the conservative book launch meant that only fifty or so friends and fans made it. It also meant that I needed to understand that writing a book was only part of the job. The other, more substantial part of creating a book was in marketing it. That would be something that I would try to do falteringly over the next year. Many Ghanaians who read about me in the newspaper and others who had seen me talk wanted to buy my book. I quickly ordered a thousand copies and kept them at my office. Slowly over the upcoming months, the books sold. I also sent some copies to my son at Reading University in England and asked him to distribute them amongst his friends and fellow students.

I also started to frequent the writing world in Ghana, visiting book fairs and readings that were happening regularly. I was lucky to meet Martin, who was a physics professor at Ghana's top university as well as a fiction writer in his spare time. As if that wasn't enough, he also ran the much-heralded WPG, a not-for-profit organisation dedicated to helping Ghanaian writers explore and affirm their identity and culture. A truly impressive and inspiring man. I went on a radio show he hosted to promote my book and discuss its contents.

All this interaction with the writing community affirmed what I'd known in my heart, that they were my kind of people—thoughtful, reflective, and intelligent. I enjoyed their conversations and perspective on life. I was now eager to complete my MFA so that I could develop my craft, join the writing community, and perhaps start supporting many writers who needed help in Ghana. This time around I didn't want to help financially but through mentoring. As I was also an entrepreneur, I could see how non-savvy the writers were in publishing, marketing, and earning money. Many didn't know about the myriad of opportunities that the internet and social media had now afforded the writing world. Through my own learnings from engaging in online courses on marketing, publishing, and connecting with the online writing community, I'd built a network that could support budding writers.

Just as I was seriously immersing myself into the writing world, that November I received a reaffirming message from my son telling me that one of his friends insisted on my number and wanted to thank me for the words in my book.

His friend then sent the following message:

> "I assure you that I am not overexaggerating when I say I truly believe that this book changed my life… It made me want to re-evaluate all of my life decisions up until that very moment… It made me want to live a life that is uncompromisingly mine."

To think, that in sharing some of my learnings I could inspire one person to change positively was humbling. My efforts, my writing, and my contribution mattered in this world.

True, there were some snide comments and judgements but none that were as severe as my own. I was the one who didn't value the life of a writer yet. I was the one who didn't think I was good enough with my writing. I was the one who was afraid of giving up his conventional life to fully embrace the creative, authentic one I'd discovered. But when I let go of those limiting beliefs with some help from many readers who enjoyed my book, writing became the spiritual practice that made me feel that I belonged to the world and the rest of humanity.

Chapter 10

A Fractured Lesson

Two days after Christmas in 2017, I fell off a snowmobile on an icy patch of slope on Mount Lebanon. In what seemed like slow motion, my daughter flew off the seat behind me while I dropped to the ground, only for the eight-hundred-kilogram snowmobile to land on my right leg. I heard a crack and knew instantly that my leg was broken, which was confirmed when I looked down and saw that it had turned to the right at an unnatural angle. The pain shot up immediately, then left, but would come back as soon as I tried to move my leg or any part of my body. It didn't help my psychology that I lay writhing on the patch of snow in agony in front of my kids, my brother, his kids, and a few other friends.

One of the guides came running toward me, ignorantly trying to get me up. I screamed at him to back off, explaining that my leg was truly broken near the ankle. Now, everyone knew that the accident was serious, and my two kids quickly rushed to lie next to me. As I lay motionless on the ground, the adrenaline wore off, and the searing pain became constant as I waited for help to arrive. I secretly prayed I wouldn't faint in front of my kids.

A few hours before my snowmobile accident, at breakfast, I'd been reading about stoic philosophy. Marcus Aurelius's words in particular were now reverberating in my mind: "You have power over your mind, not outside events. Realise this, and you will find strength." The pain didn't subside, but I was meditating, focusing on Aurelius's words. I knew that I could only do one thing: focus on getting through the pain and reaching the hospital. Looking at the anguished faces of my kids, I reassured them that the pain was bearable and that I was okay.

During those frantic first minutes, one of my friends called to arrange for an ambulance and find a nearby hospital with a reputable doctor on duty even during the festive season. Soon after, my wife came running up the hill from the hotel we were staying at, in tears from the news. After what seemed an eternity—almost an hour—two young Red Cross volunteers came with a stretcher and bundled me into what I can only describe as a metal box on wheels. The driver drove frantically down the winding mountain roads, and after a scary roller coaster ride, I finally arrived at the hospital.

After putting me on a drip, giving me a painkiller, and taking an X-ray, the doctor confirmed my worst fears. Both the tibia and fibula were broken, and I needed an operation. Again, I focused only on what was next—the operation. By now word had gotten around, and all my family and friends were at the hospital, offering their love and support. Through it all, a strong dose of painkillers left me feeling nauseated, dizzy, and sleepy.

The next day, I underwent a long and complicated surgery to have metal rods and screws inserted into my leg. When I finally came out after six hours, I saw my worried friends and family. Then my eyes zeroed in on my elderly father, who had made a long drive to come and visit me. He was sitting in a corner of the waiting room.

I asked the two nurses pushing my trolley bed to wheel me toward my father.

"Dad, I'm fine. It's late. Please go home," I said.

He looked tired and frail. I didn't want him to worry about me.

"Now. Yes," he said as he held my hand.

"I'll be in Beirut within a few days."

I grasped both his hands and kissed them as tears started to roll down my cheeks. As he got up to leave, I glanced and waved to the rest of my family and friends while the nurses wheeled me to my room.

Perhaps it was the effects of the anaesthetic that made me so emotional and allowed me to let down my guard. However, I quickly put it back up again as soon as I got to my room. Whenever there was a crisis, it was my younger self who took over.

Those few days at the hospital went smoothly as I received constant attention from the doctors, nurses, and many well-wishers who visited me. However, when I left the hospital to return to our Beirut home, I realised my challenges had just begun.

The first shock came when I couldn't get up a short staircase and needed two grown men to carry me up to the flat. This was not only frustrating but embarrassing. Then came the realisation that I couldn't do even the simplest things—take a shower, change my clothes, or carry my phone—while on crutches. I always had to rely on someone, usually my loving and ever attentive wife. I also slept terribly, waking up to take pain killers every few hours when the pain became unbearable.

After a few days of this, I was frustrated and became withdrawn; I just wanted to listen to sombre music and feel sorry for myself. My mind was everywhere. It couldn't settle, no matter what I did. I tried meditating, listening to upbeat music, journaling, and reading, but all my usual rituals didn't help. I quickly forgot Marcus Aurelius's words and all the self-help work I'd been doing for the past seven years. I was firmly in fight or flight mode, and, like a wounded animal, I wanted to attack anyone and anything. I was furious with the gods. This continued for the next ten days until I flew back to Ghana.

With a Lebanese *wasta*, it was arranged that I'd be taken straight from the car to a wheelchair, avoiding all the immigration and security, to wait in a lounge until take-off. On landing in Accra, I couldn't disembark like the rest of passengers but had to use a special lift that planes used for cargo to get down to the tarmac. All this was way too embarrassing for someone who didn't like to be the centre of attention.

Finally, I was relieved to be back home, to my bedroom, TV room, and my cat, Sassy, the Scottish fold who'd won over my heart after I was so vehemently against having a pet at home.

Things didn't get any easier at home; going up from the ground floor to the first where the bedroom was had become an ordeal. The staircase was so steep and narrow that I had to sit on my backside and lift myself one step at a time. What usually took me seconds now took me almost five minutes.

A few weeks later, things were slowly returning to normalcy. Though I hated being driven around or navigating another steep staircase at the company's premises, going to work on a daily basis grounded me and lessened my frustration. The other good news was that I'd started to return to some of my daily rituals—reading and journaling, a great source of comfort. My mind began to calm down, and my thoughts settled into a semblance of acceptance. I was coming to terms with the fact that I had to carry a mending leg around, that I had to rely on others, and, most difficult of all, that I had to sit with the idea that I couldn't do whatever I wanted to.

All this uncertainty, without control over my body or my next steps, was proving to be one of the biggest challenges of my recent history. Sitting on a sofa and doing nothing was not something I was used to. My body had always been my haven, the go-to place when everything else wasn't good. I'd run or go to the gym and power through a workout or at least take a walk when my mind was all over the place.

My mood would oscillate from optimism to pessimism. On good days, I'd read and get inspired by what Pema Chödrön said in *Living Beautifully: With Uncertainty and Change*: "When we resist change, it's called suffering. But when we can completely let go and not struggle against it, when we can embrace the groundlessness of our situation and relax into its dynamic quality, that's called enlightenment." I would then think about how fourteen days had passed and that I only had thirty-two left in plaster. Or how privileged

I was that I could afford so much help around me, unlike many others who would have had to endure the suffering alone.

But on bad days, I looked with envy at those who walked freely and felt enraged that this all had to happen at the start of the year. It affected everything I had lined up, including plans like the mandatory one-week residency at Goddard College for my MFA, which I had to cancel. Though they quickly agreed that I would be allowed to continue the MFA even without attending the residency, I'd lost that magical experience of being in Vermont. This time around it was winter, and I was looking forward to the snow and cold.

But the biggest thing that brought me down was that I felt incapacitated, unable to handle the serious problems emerging at my company. For example, we had a fraud issue at an outlet in Kumasi that needed a long car journey I couldn't take. I had to rely on others when my presence would've made a big difference.

On these negative days, I thought the concept of acceptance was a load of bullshit. The facts were that I couldn't move and that I needed constant help while the world was moving on quickly without me. On those bleak days, I'd feel victimised and ask why me? Why now? What is the big lesson I need to take away from all this?

Over the next few months, my recovery was slow. I had to travel to Lebanon twice, with all the awkwardness and effort needed now, first to remove the cast and then to do a final check-up. The doctor and physio both claimed I was doing well. But whenever I asked the doctor when I could run or return to the gym, he would say that I was lucky I was walking. That infuriated me so much that I never went back to him again. I did my own research and changed doctors as soon as I could.

What also shocked me was the reaction of people whenever I struggled with crutches or a wheelchair. On one of my visits to Lebanon, I overheard a porter at the airport tell his colleague to go and tend to the "cripple." I shook my head in disbelief. I was lucky that most of my friends were there for me, but some made it clear they didn't really care. True, a broken leg is not as major as cancer or heart disease, but it was what I was going through—the source of my pain and my misery. I stopped going the extra mile with those so-called friends, and now I hardly ever see them.

Being on the other side, that of the weak and vulnerable, meant I started to look at connection and compassion in a different way. I noticed how a few acts of friendship and love between us could go a long way toward healing each other. I recalled how the taxi drivers in Beirut would rush out of their seats to help me enter and settle into the front seat. How one of my friends back in Ghana insisted on arranging weekly takeout every Saturday so that I could see and be with everyone. How Ella and the ladies from the 'Shift Programme' called me regularly to check on me and cheer me up.

A big moment of triumph was when I started to use one crutch instead of two. This automatically freed my hands and meant I could open doors, use the bathroom more easily, and walk up or down the staircase with more dignity. I started to appreciate the little things that I once took for granted, like walking, sleeping, bathing, and climbing up the staircase a second time when I forgot something upstairs. Finally, after three months, my second, lighter cast was removed, and my stitches healed, which meant I was finally able to swim and use the pool to recuperate. My swimming technique was terrible, but at least I was moving—an important step to get back to some sense of normalcy.

By April, my company's fortunes had truly worsened, dragged down by dwindling sales, mismanagement by some of the managers I was supposed to direct, and a general malaise in the company's culture. To make things worse, our main supplier was going through a financial crisis. This meant they withdrew their substantial support and demanded that we settle our bill immediately, which was contrary to what we'd agreed upon. I now needed both the bank's help and an alternative partner.

My broken leg, a lack of exercise, and now my company's sudden falling numbers meant that I had regressed badly in my ways, going back to the pre-2008 Mo. I was trapped in a "me against them" mentality. I was angry, impatient, and afraid. It was as if I were stuck in a valley with the Herculean task of summiting the Matterhorn peak ahead.

The only solace came from my MFA programme. Staying in it ensured that I had to read and write, both of which made me happy and less conscious of my woes. Most of all, it made me feel useful and engaged in something worthwhile. A far cry from how I felt running my company.

I had worked diligently on the MFA, and my final hurdle to complete my first year was to submit a long critical paper. I had been working on this for almost a month, but with a week left until the deadline, I realised that I had completely misinterpreted the guidelines. Luckily, it was Easter weekend. I had no work, and my wife was away visiting Savannah in the States, meaning I had the house to myself for five days. Just me, my laptop, and the cat. I worked ten-hour days reading, writing, and rewriting and somehow made the deadline.

During those five days, I didn't shave, barely showered, and never left my house. I was exhausted; I slept on the sofa close to my desk. I spilled all my sweat, guts, and blood to get my paper in on time. I did all that and would be willing to do it again and again because I loved writing.

And just like that I had passed my first year. I was ecstatic. "I'm a writer" kept popping up as a headline in my mind. The first year of the MFA was not easy. It seemed like I was playing catch up all the time. However, all the reading and analysing of other writers' techniques helped develop my writing fast. The writing I was doing on the memoir was also completely different to what I wrote before. True, it was harder but more rewarding too. It was often hard to swallow all the tutor's incisive and critical comments, but my mind was now open and adjusting to what it meant to write well.

By June of 2018, my company's woes were mounting, not easing. The pressure on me was now immense. I just couldn't balance giving my all to both the second year of the MFA and fighting to revive my company's fortunes. I spoke to one of my advisors at Goddard and explained my struggles and time restrictions. We concluded that it would be best to take a leave of absence from the programme. I could return anytime I was ready.

I also decided to declutter my mind by halting both blogging and reading any non-fiction self-help books. I wanted a complete break from advice and the how-to world. Again, Rumi was the inspiration behind my thinking. He said, "I have been a seeker—and I still am—but I stopped asking the books and the stars. I started listening to the teaching of my soul." Not only did I feel badly about preaching when I was in turmoil, but I also needed to dig deep into myself for the answers rather than seek external strategies that were not relevant. I needed to control what came in and what went out of my mind.

True, both self-help and spirituality had helped me tremendously early in my journey. I became a different man, more connected, open-minded, and compassionate. However, there were some deeper failings that had gotten me to where I was now, and I needed a different way of looking at things. Perhaps, to truly hear my inner voice, I needed to shut out the noise from the outside. This meant subtracting rather than adding. It meant undoing rather than doing. It meant being rather than executing.

Rumi's words also came at a time when I was no longer enjoying my writing about self-help and spirituality. The learnings and experience in Vermont meant that I was falling in love with story and how to convey a good one. The prescriptive writing I did on my blog felt like 2-D when compared to the 3-D I was writing in the MFA. I also felt that the oversaturation of blogs, books, and podcasts in that genre was beginning to have the opposite effect on many readers (like me) who felt fed up with the repetition of specific messages in the form of "do this" and "do that."

For the last few months, I'd felt that my writing had plateaued. I was no longer moving forward but rather sideways. I'd become stagnant and didn't feel like I was growing anymore.

With all my main pillars down, my self-esteem was at its lowest ebb, and it was little wonder that I was now struggling mentally too. I was feeling anxious, resentful, and ashamed of my predicament. All the sources of my strength had disappeared. The empty nest syndrome had left me lacking the emotional support of my kids and had disrupted my home life. My company of twenty-five years, the centre of how I'd always defined myself, was now facing an existential crisis. There was also the decision to stop writing, which in hindsight was rather stupid. It was the writing that was giving me the self-reflection that I needed to navigate these tough times. It was the feeling of expressing myself and being noticed that was filling my self-love tank. Whether it was the memoir in the MFA, through which I was exploring my last ten years, or discerning big ideas on my blog, all the writing was helping me to remain sane and feel valuable.

However, in closing some doors, I allowed room for others to open. That's how I found myself sitting on a brown sofa in small room with open louvred windows and a swirling ceiling fan speaking to R, a clinical psychologist, who helped me examine my woes. Over the next few weeks, common themes emerged. Whether it was my leadership at the company or my relationships with others, there were certain patterns to my behaviour. Whenever the stakes were high and the pressure became unbearable, my eleven-year-old self would control my behaviour to protect me.

Yes, I'd grown over the last few years with all my self-discovery and self-awareness, but I wasn't truly tested yet in the arena of life. As soon as I broke my leg, with my company belly-up and my home life disrupted, I went back to my inner child.

There was also a new dimension to my thinking. I was going to be fifty in August. In my head, this meant I should've been closer to my dreams, not engaged in a dog fight for survival.

R made me see how I danced between controlling behaviour and letting things go when I thought things were sailing smoothly. I still craved power yet felt powerless, allowing the whispers of society to affect me too much. Whenever I didn't have control, I'd attack others and make erratic decisions. Why did I panic and convince myself not to write anymore? Why hadn't I built an executive team good enough to make operational decisions on the ground that would benefit the company? My controlling behaviour meant I'd always take over the reins whenever I sniffed trouble, putting my colleagues down and pushing them aside when they tried to help. It was my leadership that allowed them to be so apathetic. They had been brought up on a formula that taught them only I could solve the big issues.

The therapist made me see all that, but the damage to the company was already done. Local market forces had changed so much over the years that our business model had needed renewal long before I started to think about it. The reality was that, over the last few years, I'd completely taken my eye off the ball and wasn't sharp enough to predict market changes or effect internal evolution quickly enough. I did start working on a new strategy and direction for the company, but that would take some time to fully implement.

Meanwhile, I was more like a firefighter than an emotionally intelligent CEO. I was full of anger and some new feelings I hadn't felt so strongly before, like resentment and shame. I now felt like a true imposter everywhere and not just with my writing. All my friends were still running successful companies and were focused on their work. They didn't get side-tracked by any personal endeavours. They didn't delve into the writing world, or any other world for that matter, which allowed them to remain focused on being successful business owners. I now had little faith in myself and was questioning what had always been so dear to me, my self-discovery journey and my supposed authentic self. In short, I'd been given the opportunity to learn from and through my own pain, but I wasn't yet ready to accept its lesson.

Chapter 11

Unearthing Deeper Revelations

As my fiftieth birthday approached, I found myself contemplating my achievements. Was I truly content? Was I closer to better understanding myself, the world around me, and how I was supposed to live my life?

True, I had made great strides in knowing myself, but the setbacks from the last six months had knocked the stuffing out of me. I was more confused and ambivalent about my life than ever before. It wasn't meant to be like this when I was fifty.

Imposter syndrome was not only reserved for writing now but invaded other areas of my life. I never imagined feeling inferior in the business world. Supposedly, I'd wanted to wind down my company, put it on autopilot, and have enough savings in place to support the travelling writer's life that I'd envisioned for myself—the life of a wonderer and wanderer. The one who was materially free and spiritually connected to both himself, humanity, and the world. The one who was finally himself and walking on his authentic path.

The fact that I was further than ever in my mind meant that I needed a deep excavation into my inner self, the self that controlled my behaviour. I hungered for something big to save me. Perhaps it was time to let go of all the self-reliance and dabble in some mysticism.

While nursing my broken leg on the sofa at the start of the year, I'd been reading Carlos Castaneda's books about Don Juan's teachings and how the

Shamanic Yaqui traditions used psychoactive plants like peyote and psilocybin mushrooms to heal and seek answers to big universal questions. My interest was further piqued by Michael Pollan's book *How to Change Your Mind: What the New Science of Psychedelics Teaches Us About Consciousness, Dying, Addiction, Depression, and Transcendence*. Pollan, a science-based food writer and a sceptic, was objective and not from the New Age world. It was his writings more than anything else that opened my mind to trying psychedelics. He also had safety as a priority, insisting that the proper conditions of the right "set" and the right "setting" must be met to have a good experience. At its core, his writing urges us to take psychedelics seriously and treat them with respect instead of as a hedonistic escapade.

A friend of a friend introduced me to Malik, who would supply the magic mushrooms. We met at a nearby restaurant, shared drinks, and discussed shrooms. He had started to grow them in his own garden a few years ago but wasn't making a huge profit. We talked about life, and his worldview mirrored most of mine except that he was a true wanderer who owned a surfing school and would often get up and drive for a few days through Ghana's countryside without telling anyone. Unlike me, he did what his heart desired, not conforming to society's rules.

After thirty minutes, he rummaged through his backpack to bring out two small cello bags.

"Here are the shrooms," he said, laughing. "Also known as golden tops, cubes, or gold caps."

I took the small bags and put them in my briefcase. He advised that for my first trip I take only two hundred grams, or two-thirds of a bag. As I stood up to shake his hand, he gave me a hearty bear hug. I don't know if it was his smile, his surfing school, or his lack of conformity, but I liked him instantly.

I began preparing meticulously for D-day, which was now going to be Saturday, August 5th. I'd be alone outside at the pool area of my home. My wife and kids would be out of the country, which made it easier for me to navigate.

I was both excited and anxious at the same time. It was going to be a psycho-analytical marathon where I'd ask questions and a supreme being would somehow answer. On the day, I worried, as always, whether I'd raised my expectations far too much. What if everything I read didn't pan out with my experience?

Following my research, I took the shrooms out of the bag, mixed two thirds with Vitamin C, blueberries, a few pieces of apple, and some ice and made it into a smoothie. I downed the smoothie and waited. I had fasted for eighteen hours prior and took the portion on an empty stomach. I wanted the effects to hit me quickly and to avoid any nausea. I'd arranged soft drinks, chocolate, salted pretzels, rye bread, and some white cheese close to me just in case I got hungry. I put on some music—a psychedelic playlist I found on Apple's iTunes. Then I lay on the lounge bed under the shade of the pergola, facing the pool and the garden, and waited for something to happen.

I looked at my watch, and it was still 9:45 a.m. Nothing was happening beyond my mouth drying up, a slight rise in body temperature, and having to squint from the glaring sunlight. I put on my sunglasses, sat for a while, then looked at my watch again. It was only 10:15 a.m. Time was moving slowly. I was now getting frustrated that the effects of the mushrooms were not that strong and wondered if these shrooms were past their sell-by date. I decided to gobble up the rest of the hundred grams remaining in the bag. My impatience and striving were kicking in, even when I was meant to relax and revere the experience.

Thirty minutes later, I started to feel heavier, and the light was now even brighter. My knees went slightly weak, but I was still very much not "turned on" yet as the infamous Timothy Leary said many years ago.

Earlier in the week, I'd had an in-depth conversation with an American friend I'd met in the Paris writing programme about having a successful shrooms trip. He urged me not to try to control things but just to let go, sit still, and allow the mushrooms to do the work. Following his advice, I relaxed, and soon the light became so bright that I was wincing through my sunglasses. I also became extremely heavy, needing to consciously move myself.

As I got up, I felt like throwing up. I'd read that nausea meant fear, so I calmed myself again by remembering that there was nothing to be afraid of. Quickly, the nausea disappeared. A theme that was apparent throughout the day was that whatever I thought of immediately manifested and became reality. The effects of the psilocybin were finally kicking in.

Looking at the dwarf palm trees on my left, I was enthralled by their movement. They were dancing to the rhythm of the lounge music that blared out. Their large stems and leaves were moving, laughing, and somehow enticing me to join. Looking up, I saw that the skyline was one huge canvas of masterful art—intense and beautiful blue with small willowy clouds scattered around.

It seemed that whatever I looked at got magnified. The details I saw were intricate and amazing as if I were using both a telescope and microscope at the same time. When I closed my eyes, I felt blissful, an inner peace percolating within me. I also had a fixed smile on my face and could feel the weight of my cheeks creating that smile, something that was confirmed afterward when I saw pictures of myself. (Yes, I took selfies throughout the day.)

I wasn't aware of time anymore, but what felt like a few minutes later, I felt restless and tried to get up. Again, I felt heavy, as if I were wearing my body like a Roman soldier would bear his suit of armour. I trudged toward the pool, and the tiles I stepped on seemed larger and more detailed than I had ever noticed before. Was that dark brown line at the edge of the right side of the pool always there?

Then there was the attack of vibrant colours from everything around me, both within the pool and in the garden it overlooked. I literally thought I was seeing new colours. Before getting into the pool, I turned to the plants behind me. The luscious white flowers sprouting out seemed to smile at me, inviting me to come over to their side. When I got closer, I felt a loving feeling within me. I sound like a typical New Age dabbler, but that's how

I felt around them. They didn't turn out to be white tulips but *Mussaenda philippics Aurora*, my wife would inform me later. They had been there for four years, but that was the first time I had noticed them. Still, they were telling me that they'd always be there, ready and waiting to offer me love in return.

I then walked toward the front end of the garden, an area reserved for the orchids that we had spent so much time and money on. I picked up a red orchid flower that had fallen onto the ground. I looked closely at it but found it slightly repugnant and immediately left the orchids area. There was something that I didn't like about them. Perhaps, to me, they had become the symbol of arrogance, materialism, and superficial aesthetics—a metaphor for how I often viewed my life. They didn't have the simplicity, purity, and love that the other plants showed.

I then turned my attention to a line of small red flowers that rested on the meandering branches of small cactus tree. Again, the details that I was noticing were incredible. Where did these squarish red flowers placed on the snake-like roots come from? I spent what seemed like hours (though it was probably only a few minutes) observing every fine detail of this amazing plant, which over the last few years I'd also ignored. They were called *Euphorbia milii*.

I was now getting hot and needed to cool myself, so I walked down the pool's wide stairway and immersed half of my body. I looked up at the skyline again, and birds were now buzzing around me. Whether high in the sky or closer to me on the ground, they were everywhere. Suddenly three big scary black and white crows with a sinister look about them circled above me. They were not as majestic as the larger yellow kites that soared above them. Before I could unpack that, one small robin flew within inches of my face. All the birds seemed to be playing with me, happy that I visited their world. Just as I wondered why I hadn't seen a white seagull, my favourite bird, one landed on the green rooftop of a neighbour's house, did a twirl, and then flew off.

Again, inexplicably, it was as if anytime I thought of something, it would materialise right in front of me.

Feeling thirsty, I gulped down a five hundred millilitre bottle of water in one go and went to lie down when the music suddenly stopped and my phone rang. After all my careful planning, I'd left the phone ringer on. I immediately felt invaded, as if the world I lived in were intruding into my present experience. Anxious thoughts were now running in my mind. Were my kids or wife trying to call because of some emergency? I began to meander into a dark alley of thoughts but then remembered what the books said to do when a bad thought came your way during a psychedelic trip. It wasn't anyone from my family, so I turned the ringer off, calmed down, and reminded myself that it was a temporary trip, not a real-life situation, and that it would end soon, no matter what. The power was in my hands. Just relax and enjoy it. That's all it took for me to switch gears and feel good again. It was incredible how I could shift my focus on demand—a sense of power I'd never experienced before.

Entering through the glass patio doors to the main house, I passed a painting that hung on the wall. I stopped to look at it. Again, the colours were vivid. The painting of a young woman wearing a mauve dress and high heels was alive. It was not still but moved like a photo taken on an iPhone with the "live" feature on.

I went to the bathroom and observed myself in the mirror. Who was this guy? I examined my face and then focused on my beard, which I'd only had for a couple of years. It was as if there were another person layered over me—another person and not the me, without the beard, I'd grown up with. I was wearing only swimming shorts and no shirt. I saw that my nipples, navel, and stomach formed an image of a face that was frowning, like an emoticon. I found that hilarious and laughed out loud. How could it be that my own front torso portrayed this frown that had so defined my striving face for most of my adult life? Then I realised that if I lost the little belly fat I had, that image would perhaps change to a smile. Maybe like everything in my life, I just needed to trim the fat. Then I would get the real me—the best me.

I walked back outside and got into the pool. I stood with my feet immersed and used my hands to wash my head and body. Immediately an image popped into my head, taking me back in time. I imagined a Native American warrior washing his hands in the river of one of the great land masses of the world—North America. I could see his face clearly with coloured markings on his cheeks and forehead. He had long hair and was naked but for leather-like pants. It was like this warrior and I were one, connected in time and space. He was washing his hands, face, and head the same way I was. The mushrooms were definitely talking now.

I got out of the pool and started to pace again when suddenly, Sassy, our Scottish fold cat, came out and then ran back into the air-conditioning inside after discovering the heat was too much for her. From inside the glass door, she was communicating that she wanted me to follow her inside. I looked at her and saw a fragile animal, one that followed me everywhere, looking to me for guidance and protection. I felt sorry for her, as she was over-reliant on me, and perhaps over-domesticated. She was not her usual aloof self, a trait I loved in cats more than anything else. Out of the blue, I made a connection between Sassy's aloofness and my mother's.

Here I was now with *aloofness*, my mother, the cat, and myself. I stayed with that thought, and images of my young self popped up. I was playing alone after being left behind at home because my older siblings had gone to their friends' houses. My mother's expressionless face also popped up. I instinctively understood that she couldn't express herself because of the hardships she'd endured as a kid. She was married at sixteen, left her home for a foreign country, and never had the chance to live her teenage years. She loved me but didn't know how to show love. I could see how that had affected me greatly, perhaps making me aloof and invulnerable and leaving me craving solitude.

Thoughts and ideas were now coming at me from everywhere. I also saw strength in my mother. She was the rock that my father had relied on. For all his worldliness, charm, intelligence, and ambition, she was the stronger one. That came as a shock to me. I'd never expected that, always thinking it was my father who was the driving force. Now, I realised what many "psychonauts" already knew, that the mushrooms were helping me see things clearly.

I was now getting tired from my constant movement, so I went to lie down. As soon as I did, I got an overwhelming feeling that I was generally a restless person always seeking something to do. True, I enjoyed solitary space, but I always had to do something even when alone. I just didn't know how to chill and relax. I was always checking my to-do list and goals and considering what to do next. The mushrooms were teaching me perhaps my greatest lesson. I needed to relax and enjoy more of the ordinary moments—doing stuff for the sake of nothing. I quickly recalled Elizabeth Gilbert's Italian expression described in her book, *Eat, Pray, Love*— *la dolce far niente*, which translates to "the sweetness of doing nothing."

I was now getting hungry. The fear had dissipated and with it the remaining nausea. I wasn't afraid of what to expect next and knew how the trip would pan out with its differing degrees of intensity. Throughout my experience, I'd go through waves of intense thoughts and feelings that would then taper off. I was in control now as if I were riding a tamed horse and not a wild one. I could slow it down or make it gallop faster.

I went into the kitchen, toasted my favourite German rye bread, added white *halloumi* cheese, olives, and Zaatar (thyme-based seeds in olive oil). I sat down and took my first bite. It was like my taste buds went into overdrive, just like the turbo function coming alive when I pressed my foot on the pedal of my BMW. Every bite was as intense as the next. I held the piece of bread aloft, savoured it, and then nibbled at it with the ferocity of a Tasmanian devil. I downed it all with a Diet Coke. Again, the full taste of the sweetness rushed to me, filling me with ecstasy.

Fearful that eating would lessen the effects of the mushrooms, I inexplicably ran upstairs, got the second three-hundred-gram bag of mushrooms, and ate it all raw. They were not as rancid as I'd expected. They felt earthy and chewy like the usual mushrooms we eat. After a short while, I felt queasy, but as I had the knowledge that all would be well, the nausea subsided. I had now consumed six hundred grams within a few hours. Not what Malik advised, not on a first trip. But that's me—going all out, even when it came to having a psychedelic experience. I had to have an intense adventure, none of the softly-softly approach advised by the experts.

Now the heaviness was ridiculous. I needed a crane to move me. With great effort, I walked slowly toward the sun bed, lay down, put on my Air Pods, and listened to music directly to my earbuds instead of routing it through the outdoor speakers. The melody was unbelievable, transporting me to a new bliss. I closed my eyes, and visions were now pouring in. Some I could make sense of, but most not. Holographs, old Egyptian images, Roman emperors, colourful prisms, and other indescribable images seemed to be pouring out from the middle of my forehead, between my eyes.

When I opened my eyes, I saw that a few branches of the palm tree above me swayed and played hide and seek with me—giving me shade and then taking it away. I sat there bemused by all of it. I looked around to see that all the other trees were also moving with joy. However, one small tree at the end of a row of five palms stood still and lifeless. Its roots were not well entrenched in the ground. I felt that it would die sometime soon. A few months after my Saturday adventure, it did.

The music I was listening to contained few vocals and was more lounge-style chill-out beats. Not only did it sound richer, but I could now understand that the beats were telling me a story. That was something I had never realised before. Tunes tell stories. One tune was telling me to move slowly, another was saying I should move quicker, and another was telling me to just go crazy. There was a pause before a string of beats told me to move gently and smoothly. Keep my form like that and I'd start to move faster, not slower. The beats were perhaps telling me to get further in life, then, stating we must hurry slowly.

The skyline was now forming all kinds of patterns and stories. The image of my mother came up again. This time her face appeared in between the huge clouds. Looking peaceful, she was whispering to me, imploring me to remove my shackles, to keep revealing the true Mo. She was telling me to not repeat her mistake in hardly expressing any of her feelings and longings. I could feel her pain and regret viscerally. She was telling me that, since I was her direct heir, I could and should continue her fight for self-expression. It was our familial battle. My eyes welled up at that realisation, but somehow the tears would not fall.

As I lay down, with eyes closed, I went through a terrifying and inexplicable experience. I felt that the me I knew was dead. Instead, there was now two parts of me. The big "I" and another smaller self—the "I" that I knew and talked to all the time. The big "I" was all-encompassing, all compassion and always knew what was right and what was wrong. The big "I" spoke to the small "I" without words coming out—an instant knowing that the small "I" needed to accept his life and those around him without judgement.

Life is about living and experiencing moments. We are here to go all the way with our feelings and confront them. That's all that's needed to live the good life. If we don't confront and sit with our feelings—whether that's fear, anxiety or joy—then we are not living. Nothing matters, nothing material anyway. We are just a memory card of all the feelings that were imprinted during our lives. I felt as if the egoic barriers that I had in place went down and everything was clear. I knew things instantly. I didn't need to see or hear; the message was there. The layer of bullshit was removed. For over fifty years, I'd been masterful at running away from my feelings instead of confronting them.

After this string of thoughts, I was exhausted. The sun was also weakening, and I knew that my adventure was coming to an end. I lay down on the sofa and looked at the beige canvas material that covered the wooden frame of the gazebo. I saw a clear pattern of small squares and lines that filled the material. The pattern was repeated everywhere on the large covering. Likewise, patterns of my life by way of images from my childhood to the present came through as if I were streaming a movie. The repeated behaviours of my life were being shown to me—events that conspired in my life and how I'd failed miserably to solve them. Why did I live beyond my means? Why was I trying to keep up with the Joneses? Wouldn't it have been smarter to invest in my company or save for a rainy day instead of staying at five-star hotels, travelling business class, and eating at fancy restaurants? Was it really because I couldn't handle the discomfort, or was it, perhaps, a greater fear—of losing my status in society?

Then another thought came my way. Why was I afraid of being vulnerable? Again, it was because I wanted to show that I was strong, special, and cool—the star of society. When I became semi-famous through my blog, TEDx Talk, and national newspaper articles, I fell into the trap of pandering to people and got side-tracked from writing. Instead of focusing on the craft, writing more serious essays and books, I'd relegated my passion to a chore with a weekly deadline of a blog post. Somehow, I had conspired to dilute what I'd loved doing.

The messages kept coming. Everything was obvious and unapologetic. Boom! Cut the pretence. Live within my means. Travel like Anthony Bourdain—for fun, intrigue, and adventure. I need not apologise for anything. Materialism was for the small-minded. I'd written books and blogs about many worthy concepts, yet I hadn't lived what I knew intellectually. Only when I could be that authentic self rather than write about it would I ever be happy and free.

As I reflected, the reality struck me hard. I was paying dearly for all my actions. I was enslaved by the rules and expectations of society. Prestige, people, and society were running my life in a discreet, subconscious way. Though all areas of my life were affected, none more so than my company. The failings were obvious, and my weaknesses had a direct impact. The message was loud and clear: act as a ruthless and effective CEO, hire one, or sell the company. Only when I'd resolved my company's woes would I ever be free again. Like a sick child, its destiny lay on my shoulders and mine alone.

As the effects of the mushrooms started to wear off, the light didn't feel as bright and I was absolutely shattered, as if coming back from a long run. The plants and patterns so vivid earlier had lost their shine, and all the visuals were getting back to normal. The sun had now exited the skyline, and my quest was coming to an end.

The long Magic Mushroom trip remains one of the richest, surrealist, and transformational experiences of my life. I'd urge everyone to try it, as long as they are over twenty-five and are medically okay to do so. When done well and under the right "set" and "setting," it opens us up to another dimension. While on shrooms, life seemed colourful, rich, and so generous—a guidepost (and not a quick fix) to how we should all live our lives.

It reinforced the fact that we are spiritual beings, that there is some mystical power at play around us. Most importantly, it showed me there is a much deeper level to our consciousness than we allow ourselves to see or feel. I understood that not in an intellectual way but emotionally, through my gut, my heart, and within my bones. I know it's hard to explain this to a person who uses evidence or science as way to understand things. However, as Carl Sagan said, "the absence of evidence does not mean the evidence of absence."

Chapter 12

Confronting My Spirituality

After the mushroom adventure, the peace within me and the glow on my face remained for a while. However, the reality was that the state of my company meant I needed to act immediately. I enlisted the help of a business coach to recreate my company from the bottom up. A few weeks later, at the start of September, I travelled to Egypt to garner support from our leading supplier on increasing our credit terms and getting more goods in.

Happy with the outcome of the trip to Egypt, I stopped in Lebanon to visit my aging father, who was recovering from pneumonia and, at age ninety, was lucky to still be alive. I only spent three days with him, but our conversations remain with me to this day. He shared that he also went through a challenging time with his company at the age of fifty-three, just as I was. When the 1979 coup d'état happened in Ghana, the economy stalled. After several years without regular income, he used all his savings and sold prized assets to both move us to England and inject capital into his ailing business. He got emotional when he told me how challenging that time was as he constantly shuffled from London to Accra, often not seeing us for months. All of this happened against a backdrop of political instability in which the Ghanaian military junta followed a communist-Castro approach that made business extraordinarily challenging and dangerous.

The night before I left, I asked him, "What one lesson or saying would you want to leave as your legacy—something that defines how you lived your life and how you would want your children and grandchildren to live?"

He thought for only a few seconds and then quoted Imam Ali Ibn Abi Talib: "Work for a better life as if you'll live forever. And work for a better end as if you'll die tomorrow."

The quote summed up exactly how he had lived, his insatiable appetite for life. His love of life was infectious. Even at ninety years old, he still had more energy than I could summon at fifty. He was also eternally curious. Having barely finished high school before leaving Lebanon to move to Africa and seek a better life, he'd always read avidly, regularly quoting works of Oscar Wilde, Hemingway, and the great philosophers of the eighteenth century. He even taught himself French and took an accounting course (before the Internet), all while setting up several successful businesses. At least I inherited his curiosity.

He embodied the second half of the quote as well, always living as if he would die any day. He was a man of faith committed to and at peace with Islam. He was not afraid of death or what came next. Because he lived with death perched on his shoulder, connection and compassion were part of his daily life.

That's what I lacked. The message from my mother through the faith healer, the therapist's work, and the shrooms all said the same things, each presenting the repeating patterns in my life: that I required the faith and commitment to stay the course. I had always been too impatient, striving for instant results. Perhaps it was my need for a clear spiritual perspective that was working against me. I lacked hope and a backbone of self-belief that faith, whether that be in God as my father understood him or in some other supreme intelligence, can give. It was as if I were the lone wolf against the world, which translated to a lack of faith in myself and in whatever venture I was undertaking as well as a lack of trust in the people around me. But I was determined to change these patterns.

Back in Ghana in the first week of October, I was invited to give an online interview at a spirituality summit. The host had sought me out after my article on spirituality became popular on *Elephant Journal*'s webzine. In my writing, I'd wondered about my faith, contrasting my struggles with my father's certainty. I talked about what my daughter had asked me when she was eleven: "Is it true that you're not religious and don't believe in God?" I didn't know how to answer her then, so I made a joke and avoided the question.

In the interview, I finally offered my daughter a better answer, articulating what I'd come to understand as a more cohesive philosophy of life. I had thought about this for a long time, and the psychedelics adventure had clarified my thinking. In short, I am spiritual—and I believe in God. I saw how well religion had served my parents. But I felt conflicted about the value of faith. I respected all religions, but I defined spirituality differently than did a strictly religious viewpoint. I didn't agree with all the rules and dogma handed down to us over many years. Or with the more recent vogue tendency toward saying "I'm spiritual" as shorthand to explain one's non-materialistic or non-superficial worldview.

I found out that the origin of the word "spiritual" is Latin. It comes from the word *spiritus*, meaning "breath." Other words that share this root include inspire, aspire, and conspire, which suggests togetherness. It's when we connect to our souls and the souls around us that we feel inspired—or in spirit.

This discernment changed my outlook completely. Now, spirituality, to me, meant connecting to something bigger than myself, to some universal divine matrix in which we are all connected in some way. We come to Earth in a human body to have a physical experience. Still, we quickly forget that there is another unseen and often forgotten part of us—our souls. We remember and access that forgotten side of ourselves through spiritual practice.

Spirituality refers to the process of building a bridge from our consciousness to our souls, ensuring that this bridge is passable in both directions. I believe we are born spiritual but somehow lose our innocent connection to our souls as we grow up and conform to social norms. Perhaps that's what had happened to me. In questioning faith-based spirituality and failing to find my own bridges, I lost my way.

This connection is hard to explain. It's often fleeting, but we all know and have felt it before. It's a combination of joy and inner peace. It's a feeling of unconditional love where we feel safe, worthy, and abundant. Most of all, we feel whole; our highest priority is love. We become, if you will allow the term, part of God.

The psychedelics also made it clear to me that, whether I knew it or not, this spiritual power had given my life and pain a deeper meaning. It turned setbacks into lessons for growth—not just defeating endpoints. The visions on that Saturday confirmed that I've often felt spiritually connected in many non-religious ways. These bridges between the soul and consciousness could be moments in nature that give us that feeling of awe. Whether I watched the crows circling above, enjoyed the small robins coming close to my face, or communicated with tulips, I felt connected to nature. I feel the same way every time I stop my car to watch seagulls fly in unison or when, on my travels to Lebanon, I sit and enjoy the beautiful sunset over the Mediterranean Sea. I lose myself to the power and beauty of the present in which both time and space collapse as one. In front of me is the soulful path to God.

The biggest bridge to my soul has proven to be my early morning routines. When meditating, there's just me and the vastness that surrounds me. When I then journal, I'm with my subconscious thoughts that magically bubble up. After all that, I feel my mind, quiet and at peace, vibrating within me. All the noise from the day before settles down, just as coffee residue goes to the bottom of the cup. Solitude is not loneliness. I don't feel isolated or feel that something is missing.

Again, as part of my daily rituals, reading great literary works makes me feel spiritual. Something stirs within me when Kahlil Gibran writes, "And forget not that the earth delights to feel your bare feet and the winds long to play with your hair." The poet's words strike deep into my core, taking me immediately to that other part of myself I keep forgetting. I find myself transported to another world, a magical place where the real is unreal and the unreal is real. My heart ignites, a smile lights up my face, and I'm dancing on air, if only for a few moments.

Then there are also the larger aspects of spirituality—humility, compassion, creativity, and connection—which I've started to enjoy since my inner journey. Whenever I feel superior or egotistic, I go to the idea that we truly are nothing in the grand scheme of things. The less importance we give ourselves, the more we connect to our spiritual side and enjoy our short time in this physical life. There are many waves in an ocean. There are many oceans on this planet. There are many planets in the galaxy. There are billions of galaxies. That humble thought alone makes all my small human problems pale into nothingness.

The deeper I've walked into my journey, the more compassionate I've become. The only obstacles to my kindness are the walls that I've built around my heart. The more walls that have dropped away, the more I see the human stories around me and feel them viscerally. I can't recall the number of times that I've teared up when listening to a story that highlights our vulnerabilities and humanistic qualities.

Creativity and particularly writing have become the centrepiece of my spiritual practice. Whether I spend a few minutes writing a poem, a few hours writing a blog post, or a few weeks writing a chapter in my memoir, I feel that I need to express and share myself. Souls can't talk, so creativity is their medium. The more we allow our souls to express themselves, the stronger their voices become. When I'm writing, time and space collapse, and I journey to a place where true magic happens. When I'm done, it's like joy pervades my entire body—like I've just climbed my Everest.

Spirituality also means connection with our fellow mankind. We are all interconnected. Introvert or extrovert, we need to connect to one another. We just differ on the how. These days, I avoid parties and cocktails and instead enjoy smaller gatherings to have more powerful, intimate conversations fuelled by wit and humour. I understand clearly that when we connect to one another, be it through conversation, song, dance, or laughter, we acknowledge our shared humanity. We give away parts of ourselves. We say, "I get you. I've got your back, and we are all one. We come from the same celestial place, no matter our colour, race, or religion, and we are all going back there."

I ended my online interview on spirituality by saying, "Whether we pray in religious houses, meditate at home, read poetry before we sleep, or spend our time in creative self-expression, we can reach the same destination. The only thing that differs is the path we take to get there."

Though I believed that, I started to wonder if my own path was leading me to the right destination. Over the next few days and weeks, I kept wondering whether I could be both a successful entrepreneur and a spiritual person. Could I unite the two Mos with spirituality? I was spiritual in my writing, reading, curiosity, and philosophy but not in my other world of business and the community I was active in—the world where I spent a lot of my time. I had already built the bridges to my soul but maintaining them in the face of my work was my biggest challenge. My business—and the striving that came with it—was the thing that cuts off the bridge. It was high time I allowed nothing to stop my use of those bridges to unify both selves and live authentically from both.

I'd seen some examples of people, including my father, who could navigate spirituality with entrepreneurship, but it was mostly faith-based spirituality. Could I be spiritual in a non-faith way and apply it throughout my life? Around me, the most successful businessmen were ruthless and didn't have a spiritual bone in them. Then there were the ones who were anti-capitalism, anti-meat eating, and very New Agey who drove me nuts with their agreeableness and people pleasing. They were constantly lost and used kindness as a facade to hide their true selves.

Perhaps like many, what confused me was that, when I couldn't put a person (even myself) in a box, I'd question their authenticity and often put them down. Like how I've done to myself for so many years. I'd say things like, "I'm thinking of spirituality and seeking the help of God, only because

I am failing as a businessman." But then as my negative self-talk faded, I'd recall how my form of spirituality by way of daily small bridges had been the backbone to my life so far.

Yes, entrepreneurship means you often must make tough decisions. Yes, business is a zero-sum game in that the company's viability is what matters most. Sometimes, people who can't keep pace with that must fall by the wayside. But like everything else, doing business has evolved. Why can't we be both kind and practical? Why can't we be grounded while believing in the mystery of life? Why can't we work hard, enjoy some fruits of our labour, and follow the principles of doing good to ourselves and others?

I knew that I could never revert to the old Mo who was only about money, success, and achievement. I also knew that I hadn't reached the final viewpoint as to what my cohesive philosophy of life truly is. I was (and still am) constantly creating and walking my paths at the same time. I was self-adjusting as I moved toward it. However, I had a strong enough backbone now to accept that I could be both spiritual and make my company successful. Instead of dreaming of a life faraway, exploring beaches, caves, and mountains with my journal, perhaps fate and life were pushing me to be the spiritual businessman that I could be. Instead of focusing only on the bottom line, like many, I wanted to run my company while striving to be kind to my employees, going the extra mile for our customers, and trying to impact our community with the value of both our products and services. I also wanted to embrace the undeniable mystery of life that is constantly tugging silently away at me—the spiritual questions. No matter how I am perceived while practicing entrepreneurship.

Toward the end of October, Nader came to stay with us in Ghana for two months as he had a gap between jobs and wanted to help in my business. Nader helped me organise a company retreat at Akosombo, a lakeside town two hours away from Accra. We were celebrating twenty-five years in existence even though the last few months had felt like our days were numbered. We dubbed the day "Going for Gold," meaning we hoped that the company could reach the golden age of fifty.

We also unveiled our new vision which read: *We are passionate and committed to helping the people of Ghana create spaces that inspire them to become the fullest expression of and greatest version of themselves. Relax, dream, and create.* The vision was more sophisticated than anything I'd had before. We were no longer just selling building materials like floor and wall coverings, bathrooms, and kitchens to homeowners as we've always explained to customers. Now we were co-creating their homes with them.

The day was partly spent in a large conference room but mostly outside playing games that included tug of war, ping-pong, and a treasure hunt, all organised by Nader, who'd learned how to give employees a fun time when working with IBM in England. Still today, every employee recalls it as an aspirational day.

I'm not perfect. No matter how much I develop myself, I will always face challenges, crises, and defeats. Sometimes, I'd get it right and find this blissful state of grace, but at other times I might get swept up by the swirling dark clouds that frequent me, slip into a reactive "monkey-mind" mode, and forget that my spiritual power can conquer all. However, it's how I respond to these slips and get back into my spiritual connection that can distinguish my life.

Today, whenever I see that I'm going the wrong way—perhaps the screaming, manipulating boss I used to be or the reclusive journaler of thoughts who never wanted to engage with others—I know it's time to stop and reflect. It's time to reconnect to my spiritual part. My daily practice helps me do that.

Chapter 13

Accessing the Spiritual Warrior

By December, Nader returned to IBM, and with him went most of my spirit. The problems on the ground far outweighed the inspiration for our vision and that Akosombo day. Sales had dropped so much that profits generated were not enough to cover our monthly expenses. Also, cashflow was so bad that I couldn't pay suppliers on time. What compounded my misery was that I had to close our two main branches outside Accra due to fraud. The managers were diverting customers away to other places in order to receive commissions and creating fictional customers who they'd sell to on credit and pocket the proceeds. I had to fire them and close the outlets, with a big loss in profits and cashflow as a result.

I was constantly getting frustrated and bogged down with the inadequacies of the team and the deep hole I'd found myself in. I felt alone because I couldn't share my helplessness with my top aides and didn't have the gall to share the details with my friends. Perhaps rightly, I feared being judged and not supported. So, what was the point of talking?

I went back to see the therapist, and of course, I'd made significant progress in seeing my patterns of failure and how my inner child took over matters. Even though I'd started to identify with being a spiritual businessman, it was still hard to fuse the two Mos and create the one unified authentic person that I needed to become. During my morning routine, I'd meditate and journal. I'd feel calm and ready for the day. I'd listen to a podcast while driving, still feeling upbeat, but my mood would turn instantaneously as soon as I pulled up in front of our office building.

I was also angry and resentful after seeing younger men surpass me with their companies, something I'd never felt before. I couldn't fathom how someone with my intelligence, business know-how, and street smarts was in such dire straits. "Comparison is the thief of joy," said Roosevelt all those years ago. And he was so right. I was compounding my issues and not solving anything. What happened to all the clarity I'd felt during my mushroom trip? Or the vision we laid out so plainly at Akosombo?

Typical of someone who acts out of despair, at the start of 2019, I made a mistake in bringing two people from outside to help me fix the company. One was to help with marketing and the other with sales. Again, instead of rolling up my sleeves and getting my hands dirty, I delegated what I should've done myself—with disastrous consequences. The two consultants ruffled feathers, misunderstood our working methods, couldn't communicate our vision, and made things much more challenging for me. Most people at the company felt alienated and demotivated, and the culture that I'd built for many years was now completely broken. By June, I'd agreed with the consultants to leave. Though not their fault, the company was malfunctioning in every way. However, they were not the answer to my problems.

Soon after, I got a phone call from one of our long-serving sales representatives on the showroom floor. She explained in no uncertain terms that our problems stemmed from the simple fact that my message wasn't reaching the company as a whole—my vision and values were not being translated into action by the managers who acted as a buffer between the rest of the team and me.

"Whatever you want to happen on the ground is not being communicated to us," she said. "Take the product training. No one checks with us. Instead, our current sales head is more concerned with disciplining people for being late or not greeting him, scaring almost everyone here."

I was now seething with anger. This time, I didn't hurl the phone against the wall like I had so many years before but instead took a few deep breaths to let her words sink in.

After a few days, I summoned all my company employees to a town hall meeting without the managers. At the meeting, I discovered that what she told me was true: my managers were not relaying my interpretation of the vision I had for the company, contrary to what they showed to my face. Instead, they were infusing their own culture and vision into the company, which was more like the old striving one I had—getting things done in any way. However, unlike my old striving self, they were not as invested and didn't care much for successful results. The only thing that mattered to them was that their word was law.

As I'd lost my focus and passion, I'd allowed a few leaders to rule in my stead. Everything became bureaucratic, and "NO" became the operative word since we were focused on cutting expenses. Even special services I'd built the company on, like offering free site visits, were being cut.

A few weeks later, I got a specialist account firm to complete a three-year audit of the company's accounts. The picture was crystal clear; my company was technically bankrupt. However, this time around, it was worse than my last brush with bankruptcy twelve years earlier. Now, the company was bigger, with massive overheads, so it was haemorrhaging faster. Also, most crucially, the working capital I had accumulated over many years was nearly decimated. The reality was that, on paper, the company was insolvent. I can't say that I was shocked by the findings as I'd feared most of it, but instead of responding sooner, I'd buried my head in the sand for far too long. I hadn't wanted to face the music and had run away, hoping the problems would sort themselves out. They didn't.

When I sat down to analyse the problems, I saw that over the last five years, new players had changed the market landscape. Unfortunately, I didn't react to make the changes needed, and worst of all, I continued my lavish lifestyle by depleting the company's capital, relying too heavily on suppliers' credit lines and bank loans. When creditors and banks tightened the noose, the company ran out of working capital.

I was so angry with myself. Why had I allowed the situation to fester for so long? Why did I try to solve it with a quick fix by bringing in two consultants at great expense when I knew deep down that they couldn't fix what was wrong? Why had I kept spending and living above my means when I couldn't afford to?

At first, I blamed everyone, including the consultants who were supposed to save me, but all the inner work that I'd done had made the truth so easy to see. I was responsible for this mess.

It also didn't help that other aspects of my life were not faring much better. I wasn't writing or reading much. My daily practice was inconsistent even though I'd pronounced to myself that it was these daily spiritual actions that built the much-needed bridges to my soul and removed the fog around me. Yet I abandoned them when I needed them most. Also, my exercise regimen was all over the place. Moving and caring for my body had always been one of the core things I did well. Whether it was thinker Mo or businessman Mo, I was at my lowest ebb. I'd finally united both Mos, but I did so in defeat—I was back to the old Mo who was spiritually empty.

By the end of October, I was in a deep funk. After all the work I'd done on myself, I was still in the same place. I knew my predicament, but I was paralysed as to what to do next. Over a long weekend, I went alone to a nearby beach resort to sit and reflect. This time, there was no therapist, faith healer, or magic mushrooms.

On the first day, I sat under the shade of a palm tree. The sun started its ascent, filling the sky with an orange-yellow light as a slight breeze brushed against me. The delicate branches above my head started swaying, their leaves caressing my face, neck, and shoulders. From afar, I could hear only the distant chirping of birds. It was as if I were the only person alive in the whole world. The colours were less vibrant than when I was under the influence of mushrooms. Nor were the sounds around me as piercing. However, I was overcome by a powerful feeling of peace. A feeling that intensified when I sat there thinking of nothing at all.

A clear image kept popping up in my mind. It would linger for a few seconds and then go away. The picture that kept forcing itself into my mind was that of a spiritual warrior. It wasn't a man clad in black and wielding a samurai sword but rather an image of me. I looked strong and serene and wore a warrior's smile. I looked like a mixture of all the heroes who have inspired me—Rumi, Gibran, Hemingway, and Alan Watts.

Finally, I got up. I walked around to loosen my stiffened body. Within seconds, my mind was flushed with a clarity I'd rarely sensed before. It starkly contrasted how I'd allow my anger and bitterness to cloud my intentions. I was expanding my awareness to allow something more significant than just my ego to process my thoughts and feelings.

Though the vision was abrupt, the clarity I felt was the culmination of all the deep excavation I'd done into my psyche. The many sessions with the psychotherapist, the mushroom trip, in-depth conversations with my close friends and family, and much archaeological writing in the form of my journal all led to this specific revelation. The fact that my company was on its knees was a trigger, a call to action, like viewing a sick child wailing in pain.

It took me a few days to discern what that image of a spiritual warrior truly meant to me and the next steps I should take. The bottom line was that I wasn't serious about chasing my dream—uniting the two Mos. I wasn't willing to do the work to disentangle myself from my old identity. I was greedy and selfish in wanting the best of the two Mos. I tried to keep up with the striver's club and at the same time desired to live this simple, creative, and spiritual life full of presence.

I was self-aware enough to know that being part of the millionaire's club didn't make me happy. All my striving only brought me more misery. Yet I couldn't stop. I was addicted. The paradox I faced was that what I had to fix, the company, was also the one thing that was trapping me in the life I'd grown to hate. Living as the successful CEO of a well-known company had been my identity for so long. Success, luxury, and money were all intertwined into the image of Mo the business owner and member of the striving millionaire's club. Perhaps if I had gotten an offer to sell the company and move to another country, it would have been much easier to start afresh and live the life I wanted. But life is a teacher who doesn't give us many free passes. I'd been hoping that somehow, miraculously, the company would outgrow its issues while ignoring the fact that the underlying structure was rotten.

It was now clear that to live the authentic life that I craved I had to fix the company and accept its limitations. But I also had to do so with my new identity that included my non-faith spiritual viewpoint. To get out of this vicious cycle, I had to design my life in such a way as to allow the new me to fit into it. I had to stop judging myself and rid myself of the comparing, resisting, grasping, and striving that had affected me throughout my life and especially in the last few years as my business dwindled. All my life, I'd identified with being a successful businessman. My self-worth was dependent on only that. Yes, writing, speaking, and developing myself was expanding my sense of worth, but I hadn't invested myself thoroughly enough in that life for it to substitute for my material success. How could I? I'd allowed my spending and striving to dictate my time, focus, and, most importantly, my values.

On that day, I told myself that, though I had messed up in many areas of my life and though I was in no way living up to half my potential, it was okay. I was doing just fine. I was where I was supposed to be. I needed all those fifty-plus years to arrive at this moment of realisation. I was ready to accept myself and my life, warts and all. It became a new starting point for me. A place where I could chart my progress henceforth.

Now, all I had to do was compare myself not to my previous self but to the "me" on the beach that day. I wanted to be a man in action who embodied his philosophy rather than one who espoused it. A man who would teach only when he had gone through the lessons. A man who was focused and disciplined in taking actionable steps toward self-mastery instead of merely learning about them from the wise words of other teachers.

Most importantly, I wanted to start immediately. How we will live in twenty years depends wholly on the habits, behaviours, and values we take on in the present day. I knew that if I didn't start now, the odds were that I never would. Life is always happening to us, with or without our permission. Perhaps I'd left it too late or maybe I'm a late bloomer, but the point is, I started. As Dan Millman, a great teacher said, "The time is always now, and the place is always here."

I'd always thought that, when I achieved inner peace, the internal suffering in my mind would cease. Unfortunately, the reality is not so. It's rather the opposite. Just like the Buddha said almost three thousand years ago, "The only way to enlightenment is first through suffering, and then secondly in mastering the mind comes the cessation of suffering."

To have a spiritual and actual existence meant to live an examined life focusing on the inner life, not the outer one. This inner journey is the heart and soul of the spiritual warrior. It is arduous and fraught with much pain, suffering, and frustration. It requires much patience and perseverance. In this journey, I'd shed layer after layer of the false self I embodied for so many years. The three Ps (pain, patience, and perseverance) that I've hated all my life and tried to evade are unavoidable. There simply is no easy fix. More importantly, doing it the long, hard way is a far greater reward.

It was then that I came up with four of five eventual guidelines that crystallised my thinking and would remain with me and act as my North Star:

1. Accepting that letting go of comfort and ease and allowing more pain and struggle in our lives means more growth, presence, and richness of life.
2. Not caring about society's whims (like status and prestige) and instead focusing on having genuine connection and community.
3. Recognising that money beyond a certain point poisons the heart and that living frugally and simply means purity and freedom.

4. Embracing the ordinary and being simply useful and competent rather than holding onto the egocentric concept of trying to be extraordinary and saving the world.

I started taking action with my body first. All my life, I've been much in tune with my surroundings, feelings, and spirit through my body. When I eat poorly, it immediately affects my state of being. When I exercise hard or go for a long run, I'm transported to a place of rapture that is hard to explain in words.

I hired an online coach to help me create the plan that I wanted. This time around I wasn't going for the six-pack, but instead my goals were strength, flexibility, and longevity—to remain healthy and robust from mid-life onwards. What if I put in the long, painstaking hours to make my body a temple and refuge for my mind and spirit? What if my body mirrored my new way of being—my introduction to becoming a spiritual warrior? Again, the first thing the coach said to me was that the changes I wanted would take years and not months. I needed to be patient.

I then committed to write for at least an hour a day, to restart my weekly blog, and to finally finish my memoir. I wanted to express myself wholeheartedly. I learned to slowly overcome that initial resistance and reconnect to the feeling of joy that I'd always felt when writing.

With my company, I made some significant decisions that started me on a five-year plan that I'm still following today. In my mind, I called it "Project Smallify" because I had to make the company smaller before I could return it to its former glory. I was echoing a similar approach that many fitness coaches adopt; lose the fat, then put on muscle. First, the company underwent an expense-cutting exercise, which meant we had to make difficult decisions and let many employees go, some of whom had been with us for many years. The total count of employees shrank from a hundred plus to less than seventy. I then negotiated a friendly loan from a creditor I'd known for a long time to balance the lack of capital.

The boldest decision I made was agreeing to move my whole business to a new location, an affluent part of Accra. Instead of saving face and keeping two locations, I put the old place up for sale. That was a hard choice because we had spent over twenty-five years in that property. However, business-wise it made a lot of sense because it would ease the burden of interest payments. Even so, I was admitting to everyone around me, including the striver's club who frowned upon selling property, that I was in financial trouble. That was something my old self could not do.

For the new space we were renting out the following year, I made a deal with the landlord to pay, design, and build the inside of the large showroom to our own taste and specifications, which would earn me one year rent-free. The showroom, offices, and warehouse would now be under one new roof. I wanted the showroom to look fresh and state-of-the-art—a showstopper for customers.

We also stopped working with a long-time partner in bathrooms who, like our old vision, had become stale. Instead, we started to work with a newer, fresher brand. Finally, we created a new logo and identity to signify the new culture, modernised vision, and all the other changes we'd embarked upon. I had finally put into action all the months of strategy I had discussed with experts, my family, and friends. I finally acted in line with my new alter ego, the spiritual warrior.

The results were not immediate, but I knew that for my company to succeed again, like my body and the book I was writing, I needed to persevere and remain consistent in my daily actions toward the grand plan. At least now, with the image of the spiritual warrior always with me, I was heading in the right direction toward uniting both Mos, backed by a set of principles that I'd lean on whenever doubts or insecurities crept up on me.

Chapter 14

Achieving Inner Peace

Christmas of 2019 was dubbed "the year of the return" by the Ghanaian media as many musicians, performers, and Ghanaians living in the diaspora were returning home. As our kids and those of our close friends also came back home, my wife and I planned to host a party to celebrate them completing their higher education and becoming adults. There was champagne and great food by a wonderful authentic Ghanaian chef we hired for the event. As always, we adults drank more than the kids.

This time around, hosting the party wasn't part of my old striving self but instead who I was becoming. Unlike some previous events, we weren't trying to one-up anyone with the party. We did it within a firm budget and with a true intention of celebrating the kids, something that gave us great joy. I was now discerning my actions much more clearly. It was okay to spend on the right things.

At the Christmas party, one of my friends told us that something called Coronavirus had Wuhan, China, locked down. I hadn't heard anything about it. The next morning, I checked online. Thankfully, the news reassured me it was nothing more than a faraway virus that would be easily contained within China.

It didn't cross my mind again until the first week of March when scenes from Bergamo, Italy, and then London, where my son lived, started making the local news.

The Coronavirus was now everywhere, from television screens to the inside of our psyches. I felt anxious and fearful for my children. I couldn't do much about my son as he was working, but London seemed nearby and safe. However, to my daughter's chagrin, I summoned her back home. Savannah, Georgia was just too far away from us, and her university had closed and gone remote, allowing international students to return home.

The trip home was terrible for her. Not only was she leaving her friends behind at college, but the Ghana airport implemented new COVID protocols right before her arrival, which held her up for eight hours. When she finally arrived home, we quarantined her for ten days, not hugging her for all that time. Every time I remember how strict I was with her and how fearful I became because of the news reports, I want to cry. Knowing what I know now, nothing was worth how alienated we made her feel. As always, fear had overtaken our reason.

Even as the uncertainty of the Coronavirus had us frightened and anxious, I was excited for the new changes awaiting my company. We were preparing to move to the new expansive showroom we'd rented at Spintex, the new commercial area for affluent Ghanaian customers. Finally, I was implementing the changes that I'd planned after my spiritual warrior visions. I was now thrilled to see all the signage and billboards fixed on the building with our shining new logo. We were nearing the end of the renovation and design of the showroom when COVID-19, as it was now being called, came to our shores in Ghana. The government imposed a month-long total lockdown in mid-March of 2020. What my friend had mentioned at our Christmas party, and I'd thought irrelevant, became the centre of our lives.

On a Sunday night later that month, Ghana's president, Nana Akuffo-Addo, delivered a television message detailing the rules of the lockdown.

Everything would close, from bars to supermarkets to pharmacies. We were allowed minimal outings for outdoor exercise or essential shopping.

The first few days of lockdown were strange, disturbing, and slightly disorienting. The roads outside were now eerily quiet, and I was completely bewildered. Being taken out of the normalcy of my life felt weird, as if I were living in some future dystopia. I felt as if I were in George Orwell's novel *1984* in that all states were policed while the media was churning out nothing but the number of people infected with the Coronavirus and the death tally. To make things worse, the world stock markets crashed. The leaders around the world panicked, spiralling from one bad decision to another. There was genuine widespread fear as no one seemed to know what to do, even those entrusted to act on our behalf in making big decisions.

As the pandemic claimed more victims and began affecting people within my sphere, my fears escalated. The sense of isolation and mortality that ensued slowed me down at first, nudging me to question everything I'd learned so far. More importantly, I was now questioning the spiritual warrior breakthrough I had at the end of 2019. The anxiety I'd been feeling was not as bad as what I'd gone through back in 2008 when panic attacks would literally floor me. Nevertheless, there was now great uncertainty around me, just when I'd thought I was getting my life in order.

Even so, I felt an inner peace that I hadn't for a long time. I was scared but peaceful. How could such an incongruence be present within me? Just like in May of 2008 when I went to Lebanon to check on my heart, only to be diagnosed with panic attacks and depression in the midst of a mini war, I felt peaceful in times of chaos. Now, I felt that peace again amidst the uncertainty of the pandemic. The anti-depressants had played a major role in numbing my anxiety and feelings back in 2008. This time around, I leaned on what I'd learned over the years from my journey and my daily practice. Whether it was the knowing that being in the present was what truly mattered or the stoic philosophy that I should worry only about the things that I could control, I was handling adversity much better.

There was nothing I could do about the pandemic but wear my mask, take vitamin D, and avoid big crowds. Meanwhile, I fought any anxiety by meticulously sticking to the early morning routines that had become integral to my life. As I meditated and journaled, grounding myself in the present and listening to my thoughts, I began to see those thoughts for what they were—products of my programming that didn't serve me anymore. I was fighting back with wisdom, embodying the spiritual warrior I'd always wanted to be.

Despite my newfound inner peace, the lockdown came at a terrible time for my business. We had a lot of goods at the port and had to get them to our warehouse in a matter of days because of a deadline imposed by the port authorities. Otherwise, we'd be facing a huge fine. I coaxed the logistics company to deliver the goods just hours before the deadline. Also, we had just built some good momentum in sales at the new showroom, and now everything was going to be shut down, which was another blow to my plans.

About a week into the lockdown, as it dawned on me that there was nothing else I could do with the company, my day-to-day changed dramatically. All the things that usually weighed on me like decisions that needed to be made at work, society's demands, and my need to prepare for the future were all paused. I was finally living in the now. Even small decisions like what to wear every day, whom to visit, or where to dine out on Friday night, things that had affected me subconsciously over the years, were no longer on my mind. There was no noise to distract me, there were no burdens on me, and there were no expectations of me. There was no pressure on me to do or to be, and I was left with this constant feeling of relief, which permeated my whole being. I was calm personified.

The complete absence of distraction removed all the tension and stress that usually built up for me before the lockdown. Finally, I was living up to the tattoo on my right shoulder—*Born to be Free*. All the lessons that I'd learned from the self-help gurus were now crystallising in my life. The better I became in lessening expectations on myself while avoiding the impulse to strive, the more relaxed and happier I was. Above all, when I loosened society's grip by letting go of comparison and competition, I started to accept myself and my life. I started to truly appreciate that life wasn't about doing, wanting, and achieving but instead about who I was through both challenges and successes.

Although the lockdown period in Ghana was short (four weeks), I got to live my ideal day. I'd rise early, just before the sun came out, to be truly alone. I would meditate for twenty minutes and then journal on my thoughts. Feeling refreshed, I'd go for an hour of exercise, alternating days between working out at my home gym or doing some cardio activity, as per the plan laid out by my new coach. I would then shower and make myself a double espresso and sit my butt on the same chair facing a large empty desk overlooking the garden. Then I'd put on noise-cancelling headphones and listen to neoclassical music—the same playlist I listened to repeatedly—and write.

I'd write unencumbered for two to three hours. I'd find myself in the flow where time would just pass as I felt my heart sing. The joy I got from completing my writing task was not like some fleeting moment of happiness. It was something more, an all-encompassing feeling that encapsulated my being and armed me with a deep knowing that I mattered in this world. That I belonged. And, most importantly, that I was on my authentic path.

The lockdown day would continue with lunch and a short nap afterward. I'd then do some admin work on my blog and social media and go for long walks on the refreshingly empty streets, where I'd listen to different podcasts. I'd forgotten how soul nourishing being out in nature was. Why hadn't I been doing this before, I kept asking myself.

Whether it was being consistent with my early morning routines, writing, or walking, it seemed that all my actions were making me content. I can't emphasise enough how not having any expectations allowed me to enjoy the present much more. With my mind not on the numbers I had to achieve from my company or distracted by my social engagements, I was free to finally integrate simpler and more mindful ways of living.

Unlike a holiday, where I'd take a break for a week or two and only temporarily postpone my anxiety, the lockdown and the surreal circumstances around it felt like a permanent stop. It was as if I were frozen in time, which extinguished all my negative feelings. Now, through this extraordinary event, I was getting a taste of the life that I had envisioned for so long—the spiritual warrior's life. I was completely engaged. It truly was a bird's eye view of how I'd wanted to structure my day for the rest of my life. I delighted in the small wins of the day and accepted with a deep knowledge that life was about the journey and not the end.

I was truly peaceful and exuding pure joy, though it was slightly tempered by my anxiety about anyone in my inner circle contracting the virus. At the end of the month, I had finished most of the memoir that I hope you're reading now and wrote fifty thousand words toward the first draft of a novel. True, the novel may never see the light of day, but I had birthed something out of nothing—and creativity flooded my system.

During this period, I also came across the Bhagavad Gita, which both validated and inspired my thinking even more. The Gita is a holy Hindu text that was written between 200 and 500 BCE. It documents a conversation between Arjuna, prince of the Pandavas, and a god named Krishna. Arjuna laments going into battle with the Kauravas, his relatives. He foresees the imminent death of his teacher, uncles, and friends and would rather lay down arms and surrender than allow so much killing. He drives his chariot to the centre of the battlefield and then slumps to the ground and begs Lord Krishna for advice on what to do next. Krishna's reply constitutes the Bhagavad Gita. It covers many aspects of worldly and spiritual life, but the core message to Arjuna is that he must fight, notwithstanding the "fruits of his actions" or the bloodshed that must ensue. Krishna goes on to admonish him, saying that confusion and inaction will lead Arjuna into mental turmoil, shame, and historical disgrace. He claims that Arjuna will never know spiritual peace if he fails to fight.

For me, the Gita's message was loud and clear: *Get into action. Do what you love. Go for your goals. But detach from the results. Detach from the fruits of your actions.* We can only control our actions—not their outcomes. But we should never—never—detach from our actions. There was now a clear fifth rule that would be added to my North Star's guidebook.

Another positive during the lockdown was that I'd started to connect with our close friends more deeply than ever before. We lived close to each other and as such could easily avoid the strict lockdown rules. We'd meet every evening. With all the vicissitudes of life out of our way, we were all less stressed and had become more accommodating with each other. Though we had all grown up like family, spending the last twenty-five years together, we had only skimmed the surface when it came to deep meaningful conversations. We were not vulnerable enough to discuss our serious issues, whether they be business, children, or marital issues.

Now, our conversations became more personal, vulnerable, and joyful. We were not feeling lonely or isolated. Instead, we were alone together. We were sharing vulnerable stories about our youth, longings, and fears. One evening, a good friend confided in me that he was having a serious problem managing his child's heavy use of marijuana. I listened pensively. On another night, as if he'd led by example, I told him about my company woes. I admitted that I had to sell the company building if I were to have any chance of survival. It seemed that when we started wearing medical masks, we somehow magically dropped our egoic masks.

The more accepting and vulnerable I became during this period, the more I started sharing with friends and family. One evening, I had one of the toughest conversations of my life. With my son on Zoom and my wife (who already knew about the company issues) and daughter in front of me, I explained that, over the last few years, the company hadn't done well and that I wasn't earning enough but had continued to spend. I explained my striving affliction and that we needed to cut our expenses and reduce our lavish spending so that I could build up enough working capital in the company to make it thrive again.

At first, my son was shocked and upset that I hadn't shared this information earlier. He was right, of course, and I didn't know what to say. However, over the next few days, he understood that even fathers could be human, that we too hold onto guilt and are afraid to show we've messed up.

Though the pandemic and the year 2020 will be remembered by most as a horrible year, to me it was a time when I became clearer about what and who mattered to me and the simplicity I wanted to find in life. That simple life I had dreamt of was within reach. The great pause didn't offer me any new revelations as to the steps that I needed to take in changing my business, working on myself (body, mind, and soul), or how to reignite my passion for writing. That all happened back on that Saturday on the beach six months earlier. However, the enforced lockdown, by pausing all things business related and removing society's grip on me for a month, validated what my soul was crying out for—the end of striving and the suffering it caused.

The freedom I craved lay in the simplicity and the mindfulness of how I lived during lockdown. In living a sample of the life I'd wanted, I understood it viscerally instead of just intellectually. Now the way of the spiritual warrior started to live within me. I could feel it in my bones, joints, and whole body. I was no longer running around like a headless chicken. The striving within me had begun to subside, and instead I was peacefully trudging toward the life that I'd always wanted. I had become freer than I'd ever been. I could feel my soul smile every day. Whether it was in my writing or in new ideas I was coming up with for my company, self-expression was key to my contentment.

Again, in understanding this, I was unifying the two Mos. I was a writing spiritual entrepreneur, a spiritual writing entrepreneur, or an entrepreneurial spiritual writer. I didn't need to identify with just one persona. Whether I continued to write all my life or get my company back on track or even start a new enterprise didn't really matter. It was the self-expression that I desired.

It was living the simple and more mindful life and not caring about people's judgements that I craved. It was living the present day-to-day actions and not thinking about outcomes that I desired.

With the lockdown over and normal life resuming, I was clearer about the mindful life I wanted. I kept consistent with my daily practice and instilled a firm rule of one hour of movement, which included at least three outside walks, and one hour of writing every day.

I also could now identify when I started to backslide toward striving. When, after a week of intense workouts, I felt exhausted and my body ached, I knew that I was overdoing it and was being driven by a six-pack image I'd seen somewhere. I'd quickly remind myself that I wasn't into exercising for the image but instead for my health and wellbeing. I listened to my body and eased my working out.

When I wanted to write an article about the Lebanese crisis, just after a huge explosion in August 2020 that devastated the port and parts of Beirut, I froze and procrastinated for weeks because I was fearful of what people would think. I didn't end up writing the article, but at least I knew why.

When in a social gathering I overheard some men discussing the latest Range Rover or wanting to buy a new plot of land that would increase in value sometime soon, I didn't admonish or judge myself for not being able to do the same. At work, I'd quickly notice when I was driven by numbers and stop myself to refocus my energy on our company's values and the culture I wanted to create instead.

I'm aware that I haven't solved all my problems, and I'm not certain of how my story will end. The huge obstacles in all domains of my life are still present, not least turning my company around, getting my memoir finished and published, and staying consistent to the principles that ensure I avoid distractions and stay on track for the mindful life I want.

Everything I've gone through since 2007 has shaped who I've become and who I want to be in the future. My journey started with the early shock to my ideal world when Reda had his accident and when the bank could've foreclosed on my company at roughly the same time. Then came the panic attacks that led me to being stuck in a mini war that nudged me toward the self-help journey. Later, when I got stuck in the intellectuality of it all, running and writing helped me express myself, untying the knots in my body and the bottled-up voice within me.

When I became a mini-celebrity with my speaking and coaching, I got the validation I needed to propel me to keep reading, learning, and growing. It also helped me take writing more seriously. These activities were all doors to what lay hidden within my unconscious. The psychedelic revelations close to my fiftieth birthday meant that I started to really grasp the fact that we are not our egoic selves. This was then confirmed when I faced bankruptcy again as my twenty-five-year-old company was suffering badly. Life was catapulting me to a new direction of acceptance, vulnerability, and humanity that is encapsulated in that image of the spiritual warrior.

With my ego shattered, I've become softer and kinder, yet stronger. I'm ready to walk my true path. I finally get it—it's the act of walking that brings the most contentment and peace of mind, not any reward received at the end of the walk. With that understanding, I'm as ready as ever to become the spiritual warrior that I envisioned myself becoming.

Whether mountains or valleys await me, onward I walk.

Afterword

At my materialistic peak, despite how I may have appeared to others, I wasn't content. I had three Rolex watches and still didn't fancy wearing any of them to a party. How petty was I? How privileged I must seem to people who earn a few hundred dollars a month.

Yet I was cocooned in my own world. Just like someone who has cream on his nose after eating cake and doesn't notice it. Without my realising it, society held a firm grip on me. I was in the rat race, chasing meaningless prizes just so that I could rise on the rungs of the status ladder.

My whole self-discovery journey was about becoming more aware that we are here to play a bigger game than just buying Rolexes and travelling first class. That journey led me to know myself much better. To dig deep with vulnerability and to unlock my deepest desires. In doing so, I unravelled my identity and surrendered part of my ego to reclaim my authentic self. There were many struggles in making the shift—and a lot of suffering. But remaining true and consistent in my self-practice resulted in my ability to confront the big "I" and the richer life I wanted to pursue. More pain led to bigger insights until I finally accessed my spiritual warrior to glimpse what my life would look like when I achieved inner peace.

True, my path is not necessarily your path. My experiences are completely different than yours. However, there is a universal truth we can both share. The inner journey and a deeply examined life are rewarding and worth pursuing.

What I suggest, if you've gotten this far, is that you ask yourself the same question that Ivan Illich does on his deathbed. Are you truly satisfied with the way your life is panning out? Remove the veneer, look at the mirror, and be brutally honest. If the answer is no, I urge you to take some time off and focus on yourself. Get up an hour earlier and reflect. Meditate on what makes your heart purr.

If you are forty years old, you have approximately two thousand weeks left of your life. Just think about it. Two thousand weeks. Ten thousand days. It may only be a blip in the life of the universe, but to each of us populating the Earth, it's *everything*. How will you spend that time?

If you're anything like I was when I first began the journey into myself, you likely have a number of materially motivated goals. Maybe it's getting a better job, buying a bigger house, or proving your internal worth through some other societally condoned means. If you're unable or unwilling to part with these aspirations just yet, I challenge you to add one more. As you consider what you want for your future, take time to reflect on what nourishes your soul. How can you more consistently implement those activities into your future life?

You are worth being seen—and that starts with seeing yourself. As you come to know yourself more deeply, the path toward a more authentic version of yourself will become clearer. Be patient with your progress. As I've demonstrated throughout this book, the path is neither easy nor linear. You may at times stumble or backpedal. That's okay. Every bump in the road is an opportunity to gain fuller insight into who you are and who you are becoming. Let hope be your companion as you forge your path toward a more fulfilling life.

Acknowledgements

This book took a long time for me to finish. I wouldn't have been able to finish it without the input, love, support and patience of:

My Father and Mother.

My wife, Rana.

My kids, Nader and Savannah.

My siblings, Hassan, Bassam and Imman.

My friends: Too many to mention. But they know who they are.

My writing coach, Julie Aretz.

My editor, Kat Dixon.

The publishing team at Scribe Media and then Mindstir Media.

And of course, to all the great writers who've inspired me: Khalil Gibran, Rumi, Charles Bukowski, Ernest Hemmingway, Haruki Murakami, Herman Hesse, Nikos Kazantzakis, Amin Maalouf, Elizabeth Gilbert, Julia Cameron, Tim Ferriss and many others.

A final 'Thank You' to God, the Supreme, the Universe, whatever you'd like to call it for making me feel connected, whole and purposeful when writing this book.

About the Author

Mo Issa is the founder of a building materials business, which he has run for 25 years. He is also the author of two books. *The Shift* explores personal growth concepts like authenticity, vulnerability, and the ego, while his poetry collection, *The Dense Mistiness of the Ordinary*, focuses on his everyday experiences and feelings during his transformation. Mo's writing has been featured in *Elephant Journal* and *Rebel Society* and goes out to thousands through his weekly newsletter.

Mo speaks regularly at conferences and workshops, and he has spoken at the TEDx Accra Conference (2015). In 2016, Mo launched a new initiative, The Authenticity Project, which celebrates people fearlessly pursuing their passions by assisting them with a cash prize and a mentorship programme.

He received his master's in law from the London School of Economics. He spends his time writing and reading voraciously in philosophy, literature, poetry, and psychology. You can find him on his Substack, website, and Instagram.

Made in the USA
Middletown, DE
02 February 2025